Watch Out!! I'm Peeking In Your Window!

*To
Patricia
Best Wishes –
Shirley Lueth*

by
Shirley Lueth

LUETH HOUSE PUBLISHING HOUSE

This book has no beginning, middle or end. I planned it that way. I've included memories of yesterday, thoughts of today and the dreams of tomorrow. It's truly a woman's tale of family love, laughter and quiet desperation. You'll find no plot or torrid love scenes. You can pick it up and read any page without fear of missing something important. You can keep it in the bathroom, the glove compartment of your car, beside your bed or give it to a friend who needs cheering up. It's your book and I gratefully dedicate it to all of those people who have accused me of peeking into their windows.

Believe me, I liked what I saw!

OTHER BOOKS BY
SHIRLEY LUETH

Prayer & Peanut Butter
I Didn't Plan To Be A Witch
Bubble, Bubble, Toil & Trouble

First Printing April, 1986

ISBN 0-937911-00-3

TABLE OF CONTENTS

"FORTY WINKS DON'T COME EASY FOR MOMS"

I'm well aware that my past is behind me. It's over and it's not coming back. Still there are times when I can't shake it. Often I lay down for a nap at 10:30 a.m. and I have horrible guilt feelings.

"I'm not supposed to be sleeping in the morning," I tell myself. "I'm supposed to be slicing carrots for stew or scrubbing the bathroom or sewing up rips in the sheets. I have no time for sleep." But I do have time. Plenty of it. And it's delicious. I wouldn't trade it. Believe me I wouldn't. At least I don't think I would.

In spite of everything, however, my mother muscles continue to harken back to the days when I was responsible for a houseful of children and a napping mommy was akin to sending them to Sunday School without pennies for the collection plate.

I'm not standing here in front of God and everyone saying that occasionally I didn't catch a quick daylight 40 winks when the children were small. I'm just saying I had to be darned sneaky about it. I wouldn't come right out, take my shoes off, stretch out on the bedspread and snore. After all, I was in c-h-a-r-g-e.

"Is mom asleep again?" our son asked nudging his sister across the lunch table.

"I don't know," another observed, "her shoulders are bent and she isn't moving."

"Is she breathing?"

"I think so. You look and see if her eyes are shut."

"Her hair is combed down over her face. I can't tell," and our daughter peered under my bangs to see if my eyes were open or shut.

"I'm awake! I'm awake!" I shouted and told them to eat their tuna fish.

Quite often I rocked a pre-schooler because I wanted the chance to rest a little myself. I felt this was a legitimate and meaningful excuse. I had one vital problem. The child didn't want to be rocked. The child wanted to play with her dolls. This didn't stop me however. Scooping up a perfectly contented toddler, I patted her softly and cooed in her ear . . . "Mommy will rock you now."

"No!" she cried out desperately, clutching her dolly.

"But you are tired," I said firmly.

"Not tired."

"Mom, she just got up from her nap," an older and wiser sister patiently observed.

"Nevertheless, little children need their rest," and I hauled a kicking and screaming baby to the rocking chair.

There was very little personal satisfaction out of this type of napping for me. It was very difficult to nod off while hard-soled shoes gored my stomach and tiny fat fists flailed my face but I tried. Oh Lord, how I tried.

I used the laundry as a pillow as I snoozed while folding fluffy towels. My husband came home from work to find me in the utility room with lint in my nose.

"Why do you have fuzzies all over your face?" he wondered as he attempted to find a clear place on my cheek to kiss.

"I was resting," I yelled.

"Wouldn't it be better if you laid down on the bed?"

"Oh, I can't do that," I explained. If I look as if I'm really and truly sleeping the children will run wild. They'll cut paper dolls out of my good magazines, or spray starch my plants or run up and down the neighborhood telling everyone they have nothing for supper because mommy is sleeping ... again."

"You don't give them enough credit," he said. "You go rest and I'll watch the children. Take your time. I'll take care of everything." That sounded great to me. I went to our bedroom, shut the door, took off my shoes, straightened the covers, pulled down the shades and crawled into bed. It should have been heaven.

But do you think I could sleep? Not on your life. Funny sounds crept through the keyhole and kept me wide awake.

And I heard. . . . "Please don't kill me". . . . "If we hide them behind the bookcase she'll never know" . . . "Who needed those old statues anyway" . . . "Has anyone seen the baby" . . . . "Oh, the last time I saw her she was headed for the door" . . . . "Look, look, Augie threw up." . . . . "Was that the teacher on the telephone?" . . . "Yep, she wanted to talk to mommy. I told her she was sleeping. She wanted to talk to Daddy. I told her Daddy was sleeping too." . . . DADDY WAS SLEEPING!!!!

I whipped out of that bed, ran into the living room and sure enough Daddy, was sleeping. So was the baby, Augie and two or three of the others.

"We're babysitting ourselves, mom," our wide-awake son said. "We're fine. You go back to sleep." Was he kidding?

"Not on your life," I said. "I'll have all the time in the world to sleep someday."

And I have. But I'm not so sure I like it after all.

"A CHOCOLATE DOLL"

My mother, bless her, was the type who would rather do it herself. I was glad to let her and grew up a lazy little thing with three older sisters who often treated me with the same respect they would a pet puppy. Now that I look back on it I'm surprised I wasn't named "Fido."

There was no need for me to make my bed, pick up my underwear of wash out my stockings when I was a child. Someone' was always around to do it for me. I grew up thinking the only ring in a bathtub belonged to fairies.

This left me with a great deal of free time on my hands. I wish I could say I spent it learning to improve my lot.

Summer days were sometimes devoted to crouching on my hands and knees constructing small dirt roads for a colony of ants that lived under the old oak tree. I engineered intersections, side streets and pretend stop lights. Prodding Mr. Ant with a twig, I sent him scurrying away from family and friends, bound for nowhere with very little luggage.

When my mother called me in to wash my hands for lunch, I left Mr. Ant by the side of the road far from home and without a map. It must have taken him hours to retrace his steps and find his way back.

The next day I would send him on his way again. My husband swears this is why we are possibly the only people in the world who have ants in the wintertime. "It's the ancestors of that great-great-grandpa you left stranded in the weeds so many years ago," he said. I think it's because we have such delicious crumbs scattered about.

On rainy days, while other little girls practiced tatting and sewing, I sat in the corner of my 18-year-old sister's bedroom and read her love letters. It was my first experience with sex. I think it was hers, too. Neither of us learned much.

Oh, once in a while there was a mention of moonlight, Bing Crosby and hugging, but most of the letters had to do with her job at the candy counter in the dime store and his on the family farm. I discovered very little raw excitement in selling jelly beans or shoveling corn cobs.

I searched those folded pages for lewdness, and finding nothing, decided romance must be very dull. Of course, I wouldn't have recognized "lewd" if it had reached out and grabbed me around the ankles. But I never quit trying.

Eavesdropping as my mother chatted with a friend over a cup of tea was another pleasant way to pass the time. I overheard them discussing the "Old Rip" who owned a nearby grocery store and I visualized this poor man, torn and bleeding, standing behind his counter sacking up crackers.

I begged to be allowed to run for a loaf of bread so I could see such gore with my own eyes. What a disappointment to find him, without rips, smiling behind his apron.

I had time as a child to develop friendships in the neighborhood. A nice couple at the end of the block were my favorites. They lived alone and often took lengthy trips to far away places. The fact that I kept appearing and reappearing in their lives might have had something to do with their leaving home so much. Perhaps it also had something to do with their remaining childless.

They sometimes brought me presents when they returned from their mysterious trips. Once they gave me the biggest chocolate doll I'd ever seen. She came in a white box and they encouraged me to take her right home and eat every bite, probably hoping I'd become bilious. But they didn't know my mother. Mama was a saver.

"Save it," she said when I came rushing in with my prize, "and show it to your father when he comes home." I spent the rest of the day deciding whether I'd eat her doll feet first or start at the top of her head.

My sister begged for a bite and I shook my head greedily and reminded her it must be saved. More interested in roast beef and potatoes, my dad dutifully admired the doll and I bared by teeth to nibble a toe. "Not until after we eat," my mother warned.

This was an unfortunate delay. During dessert, an aunt, uncle and three male cousins showed up for an evening visit. I'd be forced to share my chocolate doll with boys and she was far too good for boys!

I let them peek once and as their mouths watered, I told them she must be saved. "Mama says," I gloated.

I lived to eat those words...but not my chocolate dollbaby.

"Save" became her middle name. I had to "save" it to show grandma; "save" it until there was film in the camera to take a proper picture; "save" it for my birthday as a special treat. Mama was "saving" my doll into oblivion.

Her dark chocolate features were beginning to take on a greenish-white cast and the corner where she lived hung heavy with a sweet, sickening smell.

My dad issued an ultimatum and mama declared the doll's "saving" days were over. "After school today, she's all yours," Mama said.

Ahhh, the thrill of it. I laid the white box carefully on the living room floor so the coveted candy would be the first thing seen when I opened the front door. I could hardly wait for school to end.

I learned a valuable and melancholy lesson that day. I learned never to lay anything chocolate next to a hot air register. My doll had turned into a large, dark puddle of syrup with greenish-white dots floating on top.

"Serves you right, old proudy poot," my sister laughed when she discovered my prize was no longer fit to eat and had been "saved" into a liquid death.

From that moment on...old Proudy Poot refused to ever again save a single thing.

Not even money.

And it still holds true today. If you don't believe me...ask my husband.

"FEW THINGS LEFT TO CALL MY OWN"

I can list on one hand the things I have in the house that I can call "my very own." The list includes a dishrag, the iron, a broom, the vacuum and a can of Bab-bo. I suppose I could add my yellow toothbrush but I'm no longer so sure about that. I noticed, just the other day, the bristles had white shoe polish glistening on the ends and our daughters' saddle shoes were dancing, shiny and bright, on the living room rug. So much for the yellow toothbrush.

Oh, I hide things. Like every good mother, I hide things. I hide every new thing that is brought into the house labeled "mine." In fact, I have hidden my brand new pinking shears so nicely I cannot find them myself. But while I was looking for them I did happen to run across the bottle of cologne I had tucked away nearly a year ago. Unfortunately, it had evaporated. The cologne was gone, but the spot near the third room to the left, in the basement, on the second shelf, behind the used furnace filters, smells grand.

One of the little girls suggested I carry my "good stuff" around my neck on a string like she does her diary key. Now, that would be a sight. For one thing I'd need a rope. And for another, I don't think my husband would be seen in public with a lady who was carrying an electric razor, a hairbrush, knitting needles, a make-up mirror and a pair of red mittens around her neck.

Frankly, I believe one of our sons used to hide things from me just to punch up his day. He is older now and can invent his own excitement but there was a time, when he was three and bored, that "hiding things from Mommy" was a better game than pitting G.I. Joe against the enemy.

Any mother that has ever lived in a house with pre-schoolers has developed the art of getting ready to go out in about 15 minutes flat. The 15 minutes leading up to going right out the door and down the sidewalk. There's none of this lolling about in front of the TV or having a leisurely drink or smoothing out the wrinkles in front of the mirror...like father. Mother knows that at any moment her only clean dress can be smeared with peanut butter, her hairdo cerealized and her lipstick kissed away.

I became an expert at dressing as I went out the door for an appointment. Zippers were zipped at the exact time I slipped into my coat, hair was smoothed in the same motion as putting on my gloves and I often babbled instructions to the babysitter as I brushed my teeth. I jumped into my shoes at the very last second. Only once there were no shoes for me to jump into. No decent ones. Only the scroungy, scuffed ones were lined up in plain sight. The shiny, new looking ones with high heels were gone!

Immediately everyone, including the sitter, sprang into action. All except the three-year-old. He sat there. Eating his thumb and watching with glowing eyes...G.I. Joe molding in the corner.

First we looked in all of the logical places...in the toybox, under the bed (that was a mistake-it was really bad under there), beneath the couch, between the cushions, behind the stove, in the dresser drawers, in the linen closet and behind all the doors. Then we started looking in all the illogical places. The three-year-old was really excited now. The good part was coming. Mommy was starting to scream. He even stopped sucking his thumb.

We looked on top of the refrigerator, in the refrigerator, through the garbage, under the dirty clothes, in the lampshade, beneath the potted palm, in the potato bin and between the sheets. We were exhausted. We were also 45 minutes late for a dinner party. Dinner! I looked in the oven. Sure enough, there were the shoes...no longer shiny and new-looking. They looked just a little medium-rare when pricked with a fork and crusty along the edges. The three-year-old had curled up on the corner and fallen asleep...the deep and contented sleep of a man who has done a good day's work.

As I said before, I have learned over the years to hide things...including my shoes. I have nearly reached the stage where I don't dare let the can of Bab-bo out of my sight. It is just about the only thing I have left that I can call my own. In fact, I've grown quite fond of it. I just might put it on a string around my neck.

"THE SAGA OF CHEAPIE AND CHARLIE"

We have a pair of stockings in our house that I have washed at least once a week for as long as I can remember. They remain a bright and shocking knee-length chartreuse and are as ugly as they were the day I bought them. There isn't a loose thread anywhere in their woolly bodies and to my knowledge no one has worn them in the past fifteen years. Don't ask me why they show up like clockwork in the laundry basket.

"Are you here again?" I sighed, holding this disreputable pair up next to the window hoping to find they had finally become threadbare and useless. As strong as steel they weren't even stretched out at the tops. Possibly, I'd splurged and paid 35 cents for those stockings and unlike their more expensive cousins they've resisted bleach, blasphemy and bonging. Nothing I could think of destroyed those stubborn socks. However, let me spend over $2 for a pair of stockings and the minute I turned my back one of them took off for Mexico and the other crawled down behind the dryer to live forever covered with lint, machine oil and cat hair.

But Cheapie Chartreuse and her twin brother Charlie had no intentions of giving up such a soft plush life. And homely as sin they grew as the children grew and were as capable of attending kindergarten roundup as graduate school.

I popped this pair in the rag bag and the next week found them smiling up through their toes between dirty sheets. I sent them to a sweet niece in California as a birthday gift and her mother immediately sent them, by return mail, as a present for one of ours.

"They are back, mom," our daughter groaned as she eagerly opened her package. "She sent those ugly socks right back." And tossing them aside she encouraged Augie to carry them out and bury them in the back yard with his favorite bone. Of course, he wouldn't touch them. He still remembered the day I'd carefully slipped them over his ears as he went out the door, trying to pass them off as "Doggie ear-mittens." I thought sure old Cheapie and Charlie would get their just due that day as I stood by the window and watched as a snarling Augie scratched them off of his ears and stuffed them in the nearest ditch.

"Goodbye, dumb socks," I called out. "I'll never see you again!" And I went about my housework with a light and happy heart. That night when my husband came home I saw something curled up in his right hand. "Maybe he has brought me a present," I thought. "This really had been a beautiful day."

But it wasn't a present. I'm sure you knew that all along. "Why do you leave perfectly good clothing laying around in ditches?" And my husband dangled old you-know-who in front of my eyes. "Please be more careful," and he placed them kindly in the clothes basket. They snuggled down for a long nap and I could almost swear I heard them singing. But we all know that socks don't sing.

I pleaded with our youngest son to please carry them around in his gym bag for just a little while.

"I'm not playing basketball in chartreuse socks," he yelled.

"Honey, you don't have to wear them," I explained, "just let them sit in there." I was sure they'd dissolve from exposure to the rest of the contents of that gym bag. They didn't. They came out smelling quite badly but plump and perfect, almost as if they'd had a steady dose of vitamins. His expensive tennis shoes had disintegrated and a nice sweater shrunk from pure shock but Cheapie and Charlie literally hopped from that gym bag and thumbed their noses at me.

When our third grader needed a hand puppet for a project at school I offered to sew large eye-buttons, embroider a wide mouth and even staple felt ears on the pair. "You'll have two puppets." I clapped my hands together enthusiastically. I wasn't taking any chances on leaving one at home alone. With my luck, I'd get Cheapie, the only pregnant sock in the history of man, and she'd have a litter of bright green babies right there in the laundry room.

"Aaaaagh!", she gagged. "They stink, Mommy. Our teacher won't let me be in the play if I have stinky puppets." Poor Cheapie and Charlie looked quite disappointed. I think they actually liked the idea of being stars and a possible guest appearance on Sesame Street.

For a short while, they left and went to live in a dorm room full of popcorn, blow dryers and centerfolds, coming home nearly every weekend, perhaps a bit paler, but street wise and mouthy and they shared this new found knowledge with the more gentle anklets and argyles who had never had the chance to be swingers. It wasn't until a daughter's roommate complained they were smelling up the entire floor that we gave up sending those socks to college and brought them home where they thought they belonged.

Just the other day I tried palming them off on our tiny grand-daughter, Laura Elizabeth. "They are a family heirloom," I told our daughter-in-law. "Every member of our family wears them faithfully for the first 25 years of their lives."

"Not my baby," she said politely but with great sincerity.

Oh well, I've accepted the fact those socks are going to be with me until the day I die. And I wouldn't be a bit surprised if the minute I step into heaven, I'll be handed a shimmering duffle bag that contains my angel wings, halo...and a pair of chartreuse knee socks.

"BEDS BECOME LOST AND FOUND BOXES"

Let's take the matter of bedmaking. A very simple procedure that takes maybe three minutes of your life every day. It is not the kind of thing that will make headlines, or TV specials or Academy Award movies. Actually, crumpled covers and wrinkl-ed sheets do not even make good conversation.

BUT I do not believe that bedmaking is listed as one of the original, ten best, Chinese tortures that our children say it is. It is a very simple and quick procedure, I tell them with motherly pa-tience and in a quiet voice. I explain how nice it is to start the day with uncurled blankets and plump pillows. "All you have to do," I lecture, "is tug, tuck, spread and s-m-o-o-t-h. Just don't forget to s-m-o-o-t-h!"

So what happens....their beds look as if each had a terminal case of lumps. "Who can possibly sleep in a bed rumpled up like that?" I ask, the patience and quiet quickly disappearing from my voice.

"The cat can!" one of the girls answered.

Well, I already knew that. And that's another thing. This same child that uses the most expensive shampoos, demands a clean nightie every night, bathes three times a day, uses one gallon of bath oil (imported) per bath...this same child hops into bed at night and puts her head on a pillow that has paw prints on it. Now, I like animals as much as the next person...sometimes better than the next person...but I don't want them dancing around on my percale.

I thought buying gaily colored sheets would pep up the bed-making process and make everyone "bed proud" overnight. It didn't work out that way. The little girls use them as fancy dress-up clothes and the boys prefer wadding up in scratchy Navy blankets. They are absolutely indifferent to beauty. I like them. I think they are pretty. Their father thinks they are very expensive and says he can sleep quite well on plain, old white sheets, thank you.

The only other person, besides me, that really appreciates them is the cat. She really likes them. In fact, she probably likes them a little better than I do. She had her last litter of kittens amidst a profusion of bright, fushia flowers and live green apple blossoms...popping out oodles of kittens on a foam rubber pillow. It was a rather strange litter too. They acted funny. My husband claims it was the fushia flowers and bilious blossoms that did it. He says they were marked at birth.

We have a bedspread that is marked, too. It has a history. A history that includes ambush, assault, combat and attempted murder. Also a good, old-fashioned fit. MY good, old-fashioned fit.

One day the cat got after the parakeet, the dog got after the cat and I had my fit-all in the middle of our best bedspread. There we were, running amuck, all over the quilted, polyester blend. The parakeet had passed out from fear...the cat was hissing and scratching...the dog was jumping and barking...and I was having a fit...and trying to rescue that poor, little parakeet.

I did rescue it and naturally it was in shock. Terrible shock. So was the bedspread. So was I. In fact, the parakeet, after being wrapped in a flannel cloth soaked with Vick's salve and placed on a hot air register, came out of it better than the bedspread...or me! Do you know I can hardly bear to drape that bedspread over the bed...it still gives me cold chills.

It is true that the beds in our house are like giant lost and found boxes. When someone loses something I never say "Look under the bed" like most people...I automatically say, "Look IN the bed!''

Pantyhose, golf clubs, tennis shoes, stray socks, stuffed toys, telephone directories and gum wrappers nestle companionably together at the end of each bed. It is beyond me how someone who hints that his mother is lax because she won't iron his socks can sleep in a bed like that.

Just the other day my husband tapped me on the shoulder and handed me a library book that was three days overdue. "I kept bumping my toe on this all night," he explained. "It was at the foot of our bed."

I wonder how he thinks I can possibly keep track of everything!

"SNORE, SNORE AND MORE SNORES"

For those people who brag that they fall asleep the minute their heads hit the pillow I have only one word . . . 'Phhhhhtttttt!'' Never in my life have I gone to sleep fast. Of course, there have been times when sleep came easy but NOT within seconds of lying down. I have to go through a certain amount of pillow punching, blanket smoothing and rearrangement of old bones before I can drift into a deep sleep. And the older I get . . . the harder it has become. And they tell me it's going to get worse. Oh my!

My husband is older than I am and he has absolutely no problems at all. He's a major "Phhhhtttt!" He literally begins closing his eyes as he takes off his bedroom slippers and by the time he crawls in bed he is so relaxed he makes JELL-O look like hard stone. I even begged to sleep on his side of the bed, once, thinking this might help by osmosis.

"You take the side that has peas under the mattress," I begged.

"Fine," he agreed and slumped down into an immediate sleep while I stared at a dark ceiling wondering what in the world was the matter with me. A series of snorts, grunts, mumbles and snores came from my side of the bed. A very quiet and gentle man during the day, my husband makes up for it at night by pretending he's an entire crowd.

Don't get me wrong. I'm not complaining. Well, maybe a little, but I'm quite aware that I'm a lucky woman to have a husband who spends time in his own bed . . . even if he does snore. So, you ask, what's the problem? Let me tell you. I bet you knew I would.

It was a night like any other. I was re-decorating the White House as I stretched out, wide awake, in our upstairs bedroom. My thought processes had taken me into the Oval Room where I was rearranging the president's desk and as my husband snored happily I shuffled ink blotters and presidential pencils, "How silly this is," I thought. Perhaps if it was very, very quiet I could stop thinking and start sleeping.

I reached over and touched my husband's shoulder. No reaction. Next I ran my hand over his head. He brushed it away like I was a fly. I flicked my fingers on his nose and it didn't phase him. With one foot in the small of his back I pushed with all my might.

"Well, that should do it," I said to myself. Indeed it did. As he flew out of the bed, he lost all pretense of being a quiet and gentle man. He yelled at me. Wouldn't you? In the dead of night I'd turned a perfectly nice person into a desperado. "I'm sorry," I said. "My tongue slipped." We became friends again and he resumed his "Phhhhhtttt" identity and I went back to Washington, D.C.

"Perhaps if I went to a quieter room," I decided, "I could sleep. I'll try that." Our college daughter's bed was empty and she had clean sheets. Augie-doggie looked up with a quizzical eye as I stepped over him in the hallway.

"Go back to sleep, dog," I said. "It's nothing permanent and it's none of your business."

The window was wide open in this room and a soft breeze rustled the curtains. I could hear a far-off wailing of a train as it rolled through town. "That won't keep me awake," I said optimistically as I snuggled down under a thin quilt. But what else did I hear? It was a pitty-patting paw sound on the roof. Looking out the window, I saw it was Tippy-the-cat, out for a midnight stroll and stopping by to see who was sleeping in her best pal's bed.

"Meerrrrrrrowr, Meerrrrrowr, Meerrrrrowr," she said, leaping up against the screen and poking long whiskers through the tiny holes.

"Scat, scat, scat," I cried, poking long fingers at her nose. "Shoo! Go away!"

Tippy stood fast, arching her back, green eyes wide and as her tail switched she meowed... 'I'm going to sit here all night, old woman, and watch you sleep.'

"This isn't going to work," I sighed. "I certainly can't sleep with a cat staring at me!"

My next choice was the living room couch. Once again, I

threaded my way over Augie and he raised one eyelid and growled softly as if to say "How's a dog expected to get his beauty
sleep in a crazy house?" Ignoring him, I tiptoed down the stairs.

Dropping on to the couch, I pulled a woolly smelling afghan
around my shoulders and scrunched my head into a pillow full of
prickley needlepoint pheasants. Not too comfortable but it was
quiet. It was very quiet. At least at first. And then the noises
started.

I heard something in the corner, something on top of the lamp,
something under the coffee table, something under the cushion in
the chair, something on the bookcase...a million somethings were
loose and running in our living room. And as far as I was concerned they were all gray, had long tails and a famous cousin called
"Mickey." Like a flash I was off the couch, up the stairs, leaped
over Augie and dived directly into bed next to "Mr.
Phhhhhttttt."

He told me the next morning that he was glad I'd finally gotten
a good night's sleep.

"How in the world did you ever come to such a conclusion?" I
asked through weary lips.

"Why, you snored all night!"

Huh! It couldn't have been me. It must have been Augie-
doggie.

"ETIQUETTE SERVED AT
LUETH FAMILY TROUGH"

I've wanted to write to an Etiquette editor for years. I think
it's time. I've read and re-read articles and helpful hints about
formal dress for debutante balls, how to slide into a limosine
without showing my underwear, tips on traveling the continent
of South America, when and how to curtsy to the Queen and the
proper White House protocol. None of these were of any earthly
use to me. I am interested, however, in the basics of family dining.

Where does it say in history books that children need to throw away their manners the minute they sit at their own table? Our seven were always complimented by friends, neighbors and the two grandmothers on their mealtime behavior. At home, I'm sorry to say, it was a different story.

My husband claims it was because I sat at the end of the Lueth family trough with a long, barbeque fork in my hand, ready to jab an offending eater. This isn't true. Well, it's true that I had a fork but I didn't use it. I didn't have to. I simply threatened by occasionally taking stabs in the air. This seemed to do the trick.

I could forgive the babe in the high chair who ate gravy with his little fists but was hard put to overlook a twelve year old with her thumb in the mashed potatoes. Sometimes our dinner hour seemed to last forever and sometimes it gave me a severe headache.

One of our children ate with a turned-up nose. Oh, she ate but such a chore it was for her. Nostrils flaring, she could barely get more than one pea at a time through her tight lips. Everything on her plate was too burned, raw, cold, hot, white, red or ugly. Nothing pleased her; including her family. She ate each meal in a constant state of agitation.

A brother finished before her. This particular son finished before EVERYONE. In fact, some of us hadn't even washed up and he was done, demanding seconds and wondering why the rest of us were so slow and still eating. He set an Olympic record for gobbles. I'm not even sure he chewed. "Gotta' go play baseball," he gulped, one foot in a running position. "The team is waiting."

"Sit down and eat," I ordered, flourishing my fork. "You'll get stomach pains if you don't digest your food."

"No time to digest," and taking a last crack at the strawberry shortcake he disappeared with whipping cream peeking from his pant's pocket.

Sitting next to him was "The Inspector." She sorted through her plate like a scientist. Carefully combing the contents with her dinner fork, each morsel was examined with microscopic thoroughness before being placed cautiously in her mouth.

"This meat has yellow stuff in it," she commented. "See, it's right here on the end." A tiny light from the evening sunset cast a slight discoloration on the edge of her roast.

"It's only bone marrow," I explained. "Good for strong red blood."

"Well, pardon me, but I'm not eating it." And she didn't. Augie-doggie usually put on his bib and sat beneath her chair.

Whisking her spoon like a helicopter propellor her sister mashed everything around until the food was unrecognizable and quite nauseous. She mixed corn with cake, pork with peanut butter and bread with berries. "It all goes to the same place," she said when I asked her why in the world she would make such an awful mess on purpose. She was the only one in our family that didn't go "ugh" when I served one of my famous "drag-it-out-of-the-refrigerator-where-it-has-lived-for-thirty-days" casseroles. I imagine she thought I was squashing everything in one dish just for her. Adding a crust simply made it more attractive to her.

Our "dreamer" chewed reflectively and with great concentration, resting her chin on her hand as she traveled to romantic, far-away lands with spinach between her teeth. Asking her to "pass the salt, please" might bring on the answer "I'll wear a pretty pink dress with ruffles." Waving the fork around her ears brought her back to reality but not for long. She never complained while she ate because she seldom realized that she was even eating.

Unlike the sister who treated each morsel of food like a personal friend. As she apologetically swallowed she also had a tear on her cheek. You could almost hear her sob "Farewell, little lettuce leaf, I'll see you bye and bye." If you didn't count the "Dreamer" who sometimes sat in the same spot for one meal to the other, she was the last to leave the table and apt to gather various left-overs in a napkin to protect them from the garbage disposal.

A contortionist, our youngest son ate heartily but it was beyond me how anything could travel the correct route to reach his stomach. Bent like a pretzel, one foot was on the rung of his chair, one on the opposite side of the room, his arms stretched at alarming angles, his head bobbed. It took him ten minutes to find his mouth. How he managed through all of this to keep his elbows off the table, I'll never know. But he did. He knew this infraction meant immediate fork-in-the-air.

As they grew up they did develope nice manners and when we have a holiday meal together it's a pleasure to sit at the same table with them. I've noticed, however, they still seem quite skittish if I happen to point the barbeque fork in their direction, so to keep peace I put it away for good. In fact, I'm not even sure where it is.

But just the other day our grandson asked for mayonaise on his steak and said my three bean salad smelled funny.

I might have to hunt that fork up after all.

"IRONING BOARD WINS
FIRST ROUND"

As a youngster I was a lazy thing with absolutely no desire to lift a finger around the house. I had none of the nesting qualities expected of the females of my time. I could exist comfortably, thank you, with dustballs under my bed and underwear on the floor. I didn't make my bed, hang up a blouse or wash dirty dishes. I'm not particularly proud of this, but I'm being very truthful.

My dad didn't do these things either. Mother, bless her, did it all.

Suddenly, after I said "I do" I was not only responsible for my own dustballs and wardrobe but here was this sweet smelling male person, who'd swept me off my feet with his cleanliness, neatness and the smooth freshness of his starched white shirts. I had no idea how he'd managed it so well.

I soon found out.

Two days following our honeymoon, he stood, the romance gone from his eyes, holding a crumpled shirt. With a gallant gesture he thrust it forward me.

"What do you want ME to do with this old thing?" I asked sweetly.

"It could use ironing, honey," he said.

A sensible girl, I didn't suggest he do it himself. That's today. This was yesterday. I took the shirt, promising to have it done by the time he finished his shower. I was wise enough to realize it could become a real sore spot in our marriage if I admitted that I'd never pressed a shirt in my life.

Someone had been foresighted enough to buy both an iron and an ironing board as a gift. I think it was my mother-in-law.

Thank goodness, our apartment was small. There were few hiding places. I found the iron tucked away in the back of the linen closet and the ironing board in the cellar where I thought it belonged. Dragging it up three flights of stairs, I talked to it throughout the trip.

I'm not going to tell you everything I said but the gist of the conversation covered new husbands, a mother-in-law who gave icky presents and what I really and truly thought about ironing boards.

In the hinterlands of single days, I ordinarily didn't wake up until about 11:30 a.m. Oh, I was up and about but it wasn't what you could call my bright time. More or less walking about in a mental fog, I did nothing more complicated than raise a fork to my mouth, listen to the radio or tie my shoes. Most of my college classes were scheduled for afternoons and mornings were spent in various exercises to rev up my brain process in order to meet obligations.

Of course, I'd never mentioned this to my husband when he wasn't my husband. He saw me as a vivacious companion...ready for anything. He didn't know that ten minutes before he knocked on the door for a luncheon date, I'd been standing in the bathroom with my face in a basin of icy-cold water.

But now I was paying the piper. It often works out that way. I would be forced to admit that I was not only slovenly, but dumb; or I'd have to iron that stupid shirt. My husband took long and lasting showers so time was on my side.

The first problem was maneuvering the ironing board into an upright position. There were no instructions and as I looked at it, bent in such a silly manner, it was obvious that even the brightest person might have cause for concern. I was in deep trouble and cursed the man who'd invented such a complicated contraption.

Taking the board in both hands, I turned it upside down and tugged. Nothing moved. Grasping harder, I pulled again, bending an important spring. The ironing board sprang and sagged in the middle. With an upright thrust I pushed my knee hard against the center, causing it to shoot straight into the air and click into place. My chin grazed the surface.

"I'd have to be 7'6" to iron this way," I said between clinched teeth and bringing both fists high above my head I smashed them firmly down upon the ironing board. It sank below my knees. If I knelt I could iron beautifully.

Sweating profusely, I slowly jiggled the board into a position where I could iron..only if I leaned backwards and extended my right arm without crooking my elbow. Leaving well enough alone, I picked up the shiny iron from its box. There were no instructions.

Being thoroughly modern I knew plugging it into an electrical outlet had to be the first thing to do. One problem, the outlet was across the room. I had to move the wicked ironing board or use a stone cold iron. Few newlyweds have extension cords. Personally, I feel that's a more practical wedding present than a weedy wreath with a bow tied around it but who wants to give anyone an extension cord. Not me.

Carefully inching the ironing board over the floor, I drew it close enough to plug in the iron. In three seconds it was smoking hot. I'd observed my mother spitting on the iron before putting it to cloth. I did the same and was quite surprised to find my saliva dancing on the base of tiny bursts of ballet-like movements. It was fascinating. I stood around, spitting on the iron for awhile and by the time my husband emerged from his shower, his shirt had been pressed into thousands of neat wrinkles.

It was so stiff from starch it could stand alone. The white collar was deep brown and one pocket was tightly glued shut. He put it on proudly and went to work that day with my tears tucked in the cuffs. I went back into our bedroom, climbed into bed, pulled the covers over my head and vowed never to leave.

Looking back on it. I must have been a real gem.

"OLD CHAIR IS ON THE ROAD AGAIN"

Some of our children change addresses almost as often as their socks. My husband can't understand their nomadic tendencies. "They certainly don't get it from me," he said. "I hate to move."

Well, that's the truth. I rather think, had it been up to him, we would still be living in our first apartment, consisting of a bedroom, dining room-living room-kitchen combination and bath. To him, jamming a wife, seven children and a hulky dog into this tiny space would've been preferable to packing everything and moving it out.

Not once, in our entire married life has he ever complained of overcrowding. Perhaps, he's mentioned having to haul three tricycles from the driveway, the state-of-the-roast or the fact I shot the household budget on birthday presents for a three year old, but he never felt the place we currently lived was anything but magnificent and thoroughly suited to our family.

On the other hand, I'm a chronic wanderer. I'd rather move than wallpaper a room. Our children obviously inherited my penchant for change. One daughter has switched her room three times in the past four months and this is all in the same building.

When I asked her "Why?" she replied that the new room was bigger, better and cleaner. I understood exactly what she meant. My puzzled husband simply shrugged and said he was happy he didn't have to be there to do the moving.

When our children began to grow up, he'd made an individual pact with each one that he would move them...twice...and then they were on their own. Most used up their daddy-mover allotment six months after graduating from parental management.

I have a good friend, bless her, who fixes a ham, whips up potato salad and bakes a couple of pies when one of her family moves to a new residence. "They don't have time to cook," she explained. "It gives them a feeling of home." I'd be tied to the kitchen stove for an eternity if I started doing that. Our oldest son would move every day just so I'd furnish his food.

Recently, a younger daughter rented her first apartment. Oh, she's been in dorm rooms, but they don't count. In a dorm, someone else sets the rules and has a key to her door. This time, it's a REAL apartment with a full-sized refrigerator and her very own utility bills.

She's sharing it with a friend and between them they have two beanbag chairs and a stereo. She seems to think this is more than enough to set up housekeeping.

"What do you and Cindy plan to use for furniture?" I asked.

"What can I have?" she fired back.

"How about Augie-doggie?" my husband grinned.

"We can't have pets, dad," she said. Augie regained his normal color. He had no intentions of living in a household that was probably going to serve nothing more nourishing than popcorn and potato chips. He likes red meat and dill pickles.

"Seriously, mom," our daughter continued her begging act. "Do you have something you don't need?"

"Like what?"

"We need an electric can opener and a colored television."

"So do I," I said quickly. "I also need my crockpot, microwave, electric fry pan, washing machine and dining room table."

"Isn't there anything I can have?" she whined.

"I can give you a dishtowel."

"Gee, thanks."

"You can have the chair in the garage," I offered.

"No one can sit on that old thing," she observed. "The legs are schlunky and the springs stick up and grab you when you aren't looking."

Actually, the chair started out in grand shape. It's traveled itself to death. Everytime someone moved they took it along and returned it when they updated their decor. It's been to Chicago, Spokane, Lincoln, Kearney, Nebraska and Mitchell, South Dakota with a brief stopover in Minneapolis. It's a metropolitan chair with a preppy flavor. Our daughter said she guessed she'd take it along as it was better than sitting on a beanbag for the rest of her life. Old chair was on the road again. It's become a family tradition.

It's seen a lot of life...that old chair has. Oh, the stories it could tell.

It's been with a son when he was courting his wife. It knew before we did they planned marriage. It eavesdropped as they spoke softly of their love and moved with them to their first home.

Another son U-hauled it across the nation, leaving it beside the road when he threw a rod in Wyoming. "Someone ripped off most of my stuff," he told us when he called. "But they left the old chair." Somehow this didn't surprise me and it gave him a touch of home when he spent his first Thanksgiving away from us.

It sat, well-worn and tear stained, in the room of one daughter and become her little corner of the world. "It's where I curled up with a good book, worried about my future and thought about all of you and how safe it was at home and how scary out here on my own. It's a good friend, mom, don't ever throw it away."

I hadn't planned on it. It would be like throwing away our children's baby books.

So, now it's on its way again; to a new home and new adventures. It's seen poverty, pain, cheer, joy, love, ambition, faith, hope, dispair and independence. I wonder what's going to happen to it now.

Good luck, old chair. I hope you have a happy home.

"DI BLOWS WHISTLE ON NEW MOTHERS

Her Royal Highness did it again. Stepped right out of a fairy tale and blew the whistle on new mothers all over the world. It's beyond me why she had to whip out of that English hospital 21 hours after giving birth and look so cheerful doing it. The least she could have done was whimper a little.

Less than a year ago she languidly cantered down the aisle as a bride and without fainting, sweating or changing the expression on her face, became "Mrs. Princess" in full view of family, friends and a large television audience. Fifteen minutes later, it seemed, she was expecting an heir to the throne.

"Now," I said to my husband. "She'll swell up like a balloon, get blotches and throw up in a royal bucket early in the morning." It didn't happen. I never did see her swallow hard or appear in public looking peaked. She didn't even have an overhang. My husband told me it was because royalty didn't bulge but I can hardly believe that.

It's been hard enough living down tales of pioneer women who carried scissors in their apron pockets just in case they had to cut the cord on their way to the cornfield without having a modern-day princess pull off a birthing like she might pull off a luncheon date. My wisdom teeth have put me down longer than that.

Evidently, Princess Diana didn't have a grandmother who filled her head full of stories about women who got up from the childbed too soon and watched quietly as their insides fell around their feet like little anklets. My grandmother had me so scared of moving the wrong thing at the wrong time that I resisted even dangling my legs until the third day.

It took me about five or six babies to learn that I wasn't going to lose anything important if I walked to the bathroom after giving birth.

By the time I had our seventh child I was really very tired of the whole experience of putting up a brave front and I stayed comfortably in the hospital for 10 days when she was born. Two nurses and an orderly finally carried me to the elevator and made my husband take me home.

I don't believe her Royal Highness had to lift a finger when she got home. Perhaps I would've left the hospital in a better mood had I known someone else was going to be responsible for the 2 a.m. feeding. I doubt that she will stumble out of bed in the morning after about three minute's solid sleep and forget where she stashed her baby the night before. Quite often, our children changed beds in the middle of the night and quite often I forgot just exactly where I'd put the latest addition. But give me credit...I always found it.

My husband feigned a deep sleep as I grumbled about in the dark, my nightgown tied tightly about my waist and my milk turned to vinegar as poor baby looked up with surprised eyes at a mother who would offer such a meal. Probably, the royal babe won't have to put up with this kind of thing.

Nor will he ever cut his teeth on a dog bone, sleep in a dresser drawer on vacation or be allowed to eat sand out of an old tractor tire. He might have his own thoroughbred pony but more than likely he'll never have the opportunity to catch nightcrawlers with his dad following a good rain.

And if tradition holds up he'll have his sixth grade picture taken in a crushed velvet sailor suit. I can imagine the royal fuss at our house if I'd tried sticking our sons in a sailor suit when they were 12 years old.

And who would want to be the parents of a future king? Not me. Can you imagine paddling the bare bottom of a monarch-to-be when you caught him piddling outside the castle?

For some reason I can't see Princess Di serving as a Den Mother either. Or Prince Charles pretending awe at cheap Father's Day presents. And I doubt that they will ever have to attend parent-teacher conferences.

Come to think of it, that point alone would almost make kingdom ruling worthwhile but quite frankly, I know they are going to miss a lot of fun, too.

I also think they are going to be in for a few surprises. To my knowledge, blue blood won't prevent a toddler from throwing himself head first down the nearest stairs in order to scare his parents out of their wits or from intimidating his Sunday School teacher when he's 8 or disliking little girls when he's 10 or liking them far too much when he's 16.

Well, perhaps I didn't spring back like Princess Diana after the birth of our children but we do have something in common.

You see, in the eyes of our grandchildren, I'm a Queen too.

"THE FINANCES OF
BEING A STAR"

Last week I announced to my family that I was soon to become a Very Important Person. I was going to appear on television.

They responded to this news much the same as they do when I announce we are having homemade chili for supper. They knew that, somehow, I would manage to botch it.

I have to admit that I had some strong reservations. In fact, if you want to know the truth, after I accepted the invitation I was weak with fear. I was scared to death.

Now I watch a lot of television. I like it. And the one thing I noticed right away, was that most people who appeared before the camera seemed to be unaware that millions of eyes and ears were out there...waiting...just waiting...for a bra strap to break!

"What if I can't think of anything to say?" I asked my husband.

He laughed. Snorted is a better word. I guess.

"What will I wear? Everything I have is fat. Television adds pounds everyone says. I cannot afford to add pounds. I cannot even afford to add ounces. I do not want to look chubby on TV. I want to look slender and suave and supple and sixteen."

He handed me the checkbook. "Go buy something," he said.

I was surprised. He usually puts up a better fight than that. But down deep he knew both he and his checkbook were fairly safe. He knew I probably wouldn't spend a cent. He knew that I was definitely never going to find anything that made me look slender, suave, supple-and sixteen. He knew that. And he was right!

A week before the scheduled appearance I watched every interview show aired on every channel of our television. I practiced. I practiced tossing my head in abandoned carelessness; I practiced relaxing my body in a sophisticated hump; I practiced flashing my eyes and waving my hand with a reckless air; I practiced punctuating my sentences with a carefree laugh, and I sewed reinforcement stitches on my underwear. I felt fairly well prepared. I was excited about the prospect.

"I may get an offer, you know!" I wanted to warn my family. I wanted them to know I wouldn't change. I heard that snort again. I heard a lot of snorts. One of them stood out above the rest. It was Augie-Doggie.

"Be that way," I told him. "See if I care. You're no Lassie either."

Three days before my debut my hair died.

"It's never looked like this," I told my husband. "It has never stuck out in little wads all over my head. What will I do? I want it to look blonde...not like it has a blight!" He dug out the checkbook again.

Two days left. My face broke out. "My God," I cried. "I look like an adolescent!"

"You wanted to look sixteen," my husband reminded me.

"Not like this," I said. "I have to have make-up. I have to buy a lot of make-up. Magic Make-up. It's expensive." The checkbook came slower this time-but it came. This was beginning to drain my husband's attitude about seeing his wife on television. He was losing his enthusiasm. He was also losing money.

The day before I was to go before the camera my hands began to sweat. Everything I picked up fell to the floor. I broke one set of dishes, three ashtrays, an unreplaceable antique vase and six water glasses.

My husband was starting to grumble. He wondered, out loud, how Barbara Walter's husband managed to keep his financial head above water. I told him not to worry-Barbara Walters makes out fine.

I awoke the day of the television appearance with a sense of gloom. It was like I was going to attend my very own funeral...and deliver my own eulogy. My feet dragged as I approached the welcome mat before the studio door. As I did before entering the delivery room, I paused and announced to the world..."I have changed my mind!" No one listened. They never do.

The noon-day hostess was a charmer. She was an attractive lady-an attractive slender, suave, supple lady- and she looked sixteen. She looked poised, young, self-possessed and unconcerned that she was dealing with a wreck. She reassured me.

"We will just chat," she said. "Don't worry! I have not lost a bra strap yet!" Ha. Ha.

I did worry. I worried that my hair would have a relapse. I worried that my magic make-up would melt. I worried that water would drip from my fingertips and I don't care what she said-I worried about my underwear. I had so much on my mind I could hardly concentrate on the interview.

Clutching the chair and mumbling into the microphone I managed to fill airtime without completely disgracing my family. They told me later that Augie Doggie snickered a couple of times and the television blanked out once but that, on a whole, it was OK. I have not heard from any Executive Producers...I don't know how they liked it.

My husband told me he was proud of me. "You did fine," he said. "You looked real pretty. How would you like to go out for dinner to celebrate!"

Out came the checkbook again. My, it can become expensive when you are a star!

"WHEN CAR REPAIRS DON'T PAY"

Our station wagon just died. I do not plan to pay its funeral expenses.

True, it has been a trusted family companion for lo, these many years and each dent, gouge and scratch was lovingly put there by its best friend...me! And yes, I have caused its hood to turn white and its windshield wipers to flex in fright as I rounded a corner that wasn't there and yes, quite often, it did have to park under its own power while I was doing something else...but nevertheless, even in the closest of relationships, sometimes it is wise to cut the ties.

"I talked to the man at the garage," I told my husband, "he said he didn't think the station wagon could possibly stand up under one more sideswipe. To get it running again would take an awful lot of effort by an awful lot of people. I don't think it is worth it. I think I'd like a new car to drive."

The children reacted just as I thought they would. "Wow! A new car!" our youngest son yelled, "Buy a van, mom. Don't just get a car. Van's are in. Plush ones. Get one with blue shag carpeting and candelabra and soft cushions and mirrors."

The thought made me blush. I told him I didn't think a van like that was what I had in mind. Can you imagine the reaction of the carry-out boy at the grocery store? Creamed corn and candles definitely don't belong together.

"Mother, mother, don't get a van," our daughter suggested. "For some reason I can't imagine you in a van." I couldn't either...for the same reason. "Now, I see you in a lipstick red, low-slung sports car with bucket seats and four-on-the-floor."

I couldn't even fit into one of those.

And the thought of running into a mailbox in a car that weighs less than I do gave me the shivers. I could possibly destroy myself in less than two hours in a small sports car.

"I don't think so," I said. My husband looked very relieved.

"Buy a pick-up," our oldest son volunteered hopefully, "and a dog and a shotgun."

"If I bought a pick-up," I pointed out, "I would have to live in it forever. Pickups are very hard to climb into and out of without muscle cramps. I could climb in, perhaps, but I have grave doubts that I would ever get out again. You have to be a latent mountain-climber to own a pickup. And you know I don't like guns...and we already have a dog."

"But Augie won't ride with you."

"That is his problem."

"Why don't you just go pick out a good used car," my husband said...stressing the word "used." The word "new" is not in his vocabulary.

"I know nothing about cars," I admitted. "You know that."

"It is time you learned," he said. And that was the end of that!

No one was around when I entered the display room of the motor company. By some strange and odd coincidence the whole group of working men were huddled in the grease pit, hiding behind a large oil drum.

"Yoo-hoo," I yelled. "I want to buy a car. Will someone help me?"

I could see a hustle and bustle among the men. They were flipping a coin. One lost. He was elected to sell me a car. He had a funny look on his face. Trapped might be a good description.

Now I had done some homework before I entered that building. I had no intentions of letting that salesman think he was dealing with a patsy. I walked around the lot looking superior and kicking tires. I had clipped an ad from the paper and memorized the terminology.

"What I am really looking for," I said crisply, "is a one-owner hardtop, with power steering, brakes and air, fantastic mileage, magnum headers, new radial tires, tilt, extra sharp and clean."

"How much would you like to pay for it," he asked. He seemed impressed.

"Would $75 do it?" I asked.

The salesman looked longingly toward the pit and asked me three questions...(1) Does your husband know you are here? (2) Can you really and truly drive? and (3) Do you have a dog? And then he showed me a car.

He flipped open the hood and I looked in. It appeared to have everything in there a car was supposed to have.

"I'll take it," I said firmly and just like that I was the owner of a car. I was so proud. I could hardly wait to run home and call my husband.

"What kind is it?" he asked.

"It is green and has four wheels. It goes backward and forward"...and as far as I was concerned that was adequate and all I needed to know. After all, the car didn't ask me about MY background...and that suited me fine.

What that car doesn't know...won't hurt it!

"CASE OF BASEMENT BARBER"

Our daughters began to ignore television, radio, dog, cats, brothers, sisters, mother and father when they were about 15 or 16 and took up hair-combing as a hobby.

I warned them if they continued plowing their scalps every three minutes with a fine-toothed comb their hair would start falling out by the roots. Long, straight hair appeared on the soap, soap dish, sink, vanity table, in the medicine cabinet, on the begonia plant, wound around the shampoo bottle, twisted in the woodwork and cuddled quietly on the light fixtures. It was like entering a forest.

Our oldest son gagged every time he brushed his teeth (voluntarily about every six weeks) and claimed he'd rather have cavities than die of hair balls in his stomach. My husband insisted they were all going to be bald before they were 18 and more than likely he would end up with five unmarried daughters with no hair and they would have to live with us the rest of their lives and he would never get a chance to shower or shave again as long as he lived.

I told him he exaggerated and wasn't he glad the girls chose to be neat and nice instead of smelling like old wool and having their hair buzzed off like the boy's. This, of course, was a few years ago when our sons were younger and had crew cuts and didn't use blow dryers, hot combs, curling irons, bobby pins or have perms.

And they didn't drop hair in the house because they didn't have any. Their father saw to that. Once a month, or more, depending on the weather and if they were playing baseball, he took them to the basement and politely and swiftly sheared their heads to the nubbin. Augie-Doggie left home periodically and visited strangers so he wouldn't fall under the clipper and I didn't hang around a lot either. The girls were terrified.

My husband was definitely into home barbering and he took it seriously. His tools were as honed and polished as any surgeon's instruments. I expected, at any time, to be called upon to stand by his side, made to wear a sterilized green gown, mask and cloth cap while slapping comb and brush into his palm.

When the boys were younger they really didn't mind having their hair cut by their Dad and set tall and straight on the high stool and let him cut every hair on their head down to a mere patch scattered at random over their skulls. Ears stood out straight from their heads and their eyes looked hollow. Their grandmother thought they were constantly ill and offered to buy vitamins. I told her it was their haircuts but she didn't believe me.

Sometimes even my husband had to admit they looked pretty awful but he said it was a practical way to keep them neat and clean and it was sure easy to comb. In fact, it was impossible to comb because there was nothing there. Their older sisters made fun of them and a younger sister thought, for years, the only difference between a boy and a girl was the haircut. And it was comfortable in the summer.

True, during the winter, they ran the danger of developing chilblains on top of their heads but I made them wear heavy, tight, fat stocking caps that mashed their ears flat and left ridges on their foreheads. They complained of this far more than they did their dad's haircuts.

And it was practical...very practical. So practical I told my husband I thought it would be an excellent idea if he would just let me cut his hair once in awhile and then he wouldn't have to worry about a barber and we could save enough money to hire a babysitter and stay overnight in a motel once in awhile. With that prospect in mind, he reluctantly consented. I really didn't think it would be hard. After all I had watched and it seemed easy enough. It couldn't be much different than cutting out a dress pattern with a pair of electric scissors. Just substitute the contours of the head for the black outlines of the pattern and zip right along. I was wrong. I didn't take into account that the head would move when I knicked an ear causing the contours to resemble a rocky road and the hair to end up invisible in certain spots after being slashed.

"You've cut my hair off in sections," my husband yelled. "I look like a partially, psychopathic Kojak. And my ear's bleeding. How can I go to work like this?" I thought he was going to cry.

"Wear a stocking cap, Dad. That's what she makes us do."

"I won't wear a stocking cap," he said firmly.

"Would you wear a turban?" I giggled. "It would make you seem foreign, mysterious and quite handsome." Of course he wouldn't wear a turban. I hadn't really expected him too. And that was the very last time he would ever let me cut his hair and then one day, one son entered junior high and declared that only Marines wore their hair cut so short and only poor people had their hair cut at home and the other brother agreed and we entered the period in time when the boys wore their hair as long as the girls and I began to worry that perhaps they would never marry and would spend the rest of their lives living with us.

Neither boy would stay more than three minutes at a time with their Dad in the basement...alone...for fear he would cut their hair under parental force. The barbering tools were tucked sadly away behind the barrel with the baby clothes and left to rust and grow dull. However, just the other day my husband looked at our little grandson and wistfully said "Don't you think he needs a haircut?" and the baby was immediately snatched up and taken home by his mother before grandpa got any ideas. She wasn't taking any chances.

"A BARGAIN AT ANY PRICE"

Boy, I just went through an "experience" and there's no doubt about it...only the stalwart survived. I went to a sale.

And what a sale! Everything from toilet seats to chicken pot pie was up for grabs. And grab we did. I've never had so much fun in my life. Of course, my husband still hasn't spoken to me because I lost him somewhere in housewares and before he could say "Where am I?" he'd bought three vegetable steamers and a vacuum cleaner. I didn't see him again for two hours. He looked four inches shorter and twenty years older and didn't stop shaking until I had him home, dressed in his jamies and sitting in his favorite chair with a hot drink in his hand.

"I've never seen anything like it." he said, his eyes slightly crossed. "I stood in line for 30 minutes to buy a pair of pants that weren't even on sale. I don't know what came over me." I do. And isn't it wonderful!

It's a fact of life that the words "marked down" does something to a person and I saw hundreds of husbands, lured by wives who said "I just want to look a little" and tiny tots who thought they were going to McDonald's for supper, thrown in the middle of a group of women...all with 14 hands...out for a bargain.

"I haven't been this close to an invasion since Guadacanal," groaned a white haired man who cowered on the edge of the store aisle carrying 82 shopping bags. The portly gentleman looked terrified and kept getting his feet stomped. I had the feeling that before the night was over he was going to wish with all his heart he was back in the safe warmth of a WW2 foxhole.

It took all my willpower to keep from buying three pair of Calvin Klein jeans because they were reduced $10. I couldn't draw those jeans up over my ankles but because the temptation was so great I found myself standing in line at the cash register with those jeans in my arms.

Behind me a petite lady in her 70s had a maternity smock clutched in wrinkled hands. "One-half off," she quivered. Thank goodness both of us woke up just in time to put that stuff back before paying cash.

"That was close!" she said, wiping away the nervous perspiration. "I'd never have been able to explain that to my husband." I knew just where she was coming from.

Breathless and limp because I'd just been saved from a purchase I couldn't have gotten into with a can opener I went outside the store to catch my breath and re-group. It took me almost an hour to fight my way to the front door and naturally I couldn't resist a bit of shopping.

I bought an oversized canvas tote bag with a smiling green frog on it, six pair of woolly leg warmers and a straw hat. God only knows what I'll do with them, but believe me when I say they were a real steal.

Once I reached the outside of the store I had the choice of sitting down on the floor of the mall or curling up next to a giant potted plant. Every available seat was taken by (1) Men reading newspapers (2) Tired women with their heads between their legs (3)Sleeping babies. Standing on one leg I wondered why one earth I'd chosen this particular time to wear shoes with three inch heels. Who needs to look nice to push and shove?

The real pros were dressed in tennis shoes and pre-torn blouses. Standing there like a fat flamingo with a straw hat clenched in its teeth, I watched as a young father with two crying preschoolers came near. "Where's mommy?" the little girl screamed.

"She's in THERE!" he said in the same tone of voice that might have described his wife sitting down to dinner with the devil.

"Want my mommy," the small child continued to sob. Her brother took up the wail. Fighting back his own tears, the daddy squared his shoulders and prepared to enter the store.

"I wouldn't go in there if I were you," I warned. "If you let go of their hands for an instant you'll never find those babies again."

"I have to find my wife," he said. "My daughter has to go potty and I certainly can't take her. She went in there to buy a spool of thread and I haven't seen her for three hours." And you may well never see her again, I thought, remembering my own husband swallowed up by cannisters and cleaning equipment. After explaining to the poor man that I was the mother of seven, grandmother of five, who smoked some, took an occasional social drink but was totally reliable and harmless, I told him if he'd hold my packages I'd take the little girl to the bathroom. He reached out for the straw hat and leg warmers but told me I'd have to carry the bag with the frog.

A cute three year old, the tiny girl gladly took my hand. At this point I think she would've gone with King Kong, and the two of us went to the nearest restroom. In order to make conversation I asked her what they'd been doing while mommy shopped.

"Oh," she said, "We went to this big room that had lots of smoke and loud music and a pretty lady brought daddy a pitcher of beer and my brother and I had pop and corn curls for supper and daddy said he'd give us a quarter if we'd tell mommy we'd been sitting in the car all the time she was lost in the store."

When I returned the little girl to her daddy, her mother had joined them and her brother had a quarter in his hand. I said "see you" and turned to go. The little girl pulled at my sleeve and said softly..."Can I kiss you good-bye, lady?"

Who needs Calvin Kleins? I'd just gotten the best bargain of the night.

"GRANDMA'S RULES"

For 13 years my husband and I have been grandparents. Sometimes this comes as a surprise when I discover I'm not yet living the life of a rich and famous person. I figure if an individual hasn't made it by the time they are a grandma, chances are it isn't going to happen. Never mind, it's more fun being a grandma anyway. Take it from me...I know.

Being a grandparent is like a comfortable warm sweater on a cold, cold night. Nothing can hold a candle to it. No references are required and you don't have to be thin. I especially like that part. Of course, having children of your own is necessary but these children don't have to be smart, beautiful or even co-operative. Don't worry. Flaws don't rub off on grandchildren. For some reason...they are always perfect and remain that way..even when they are in Junior High.

Perhaps the following rules for grandparenthood won't hold true for everyone but I've found them most useful:

(1) Strong nerves and a large portable cookie jar are essential. The strong nerves will come in handy while traveling with grandchildren on educational trips to the zoo, museum or local hamburger joint. All those under eight could whine a bit and fuss; over eight will claim they are bored and could resort to punching out whoever is close. Feeding them cookies might keep peace and prevent grandpa from running into a tree while shouting "Can't you keep things under control" at grandma.

(2) Any meal served to visiting grandchildren can be made edible by omitting spinach and substituting french fries.

(3) While shopping for grandchildren on birthdays, Christmas, Easter, Valentine's Day, Fourth of July, Groundhog's Day, Washington's Birthday and the third Thursday of every month, it isn't necessary for grandpa to stand around the store shuffling his feet, clasping his billfold and looking like a sour goose. Grandpa must learn he can't take it with him.

(4) A telephone call or handwritten note that begins..."We were wondering if you were busy this weekend..." means you'd better run put the toilet bowl cleanser on the top shelf, your best porcelain figurine in a safe place and warn the cat. Grandma and Grandpa are going to have company.

(5) You must learn to shrug off comments like "Why are your teeth yellow, Grandma?" and "You have a fat stomach, Grandpa." You don't have to explain to this precious child that not only are Grandma's teeth yellow, they sleep in a cup. Or that Grandpa's stomach was once his chest and shoulders.

(6) Grandchildren always forgive grandparents for looking funny. It's my favorite rule.

(7) When they say "My mommy doesn't make me take a nap!" refrain from telling them their mommy is obviously a poop. Patiently bribe them by promising ice cream and candy bars when Grandma wakes up from HER nap.

(8) Try and be a good sport when a favorite soap opera is replaced by Seasame Street and/or Mr. Rogers. True, Mr. Rogers tippytoeing around in his sweater doesn't replace love in the afternoon but if you're a grandparent more than likely you've had your fair share of love in the afternoon anyway. Trust me. Sixty minutes of peace and quiet while grandchildren watch cartoons can be more gratifying then romance.

(9) When a grandson has a hammer lock on a little sister try not to interfere. Old bones heal slowly.

(10) Popcorn, peanut butter, gumdrops and lollipops are cheaper when bought by the gross.

(11) Never throw anything away. Grandchildren love junk. For

example, a shower cap makes a marvelous space helmet; left-over yarn can be turned into pretty bows for tiny pigtails and a half empty bottle of old perfume can stink up a sweet granddaughter for days.

(12) A "hurty" deserves great doses of ointment, the biggest bandage in the house, a dime, several kisses and a march down memory lane as grandma explains that her/his mommy/daddy cried buckets the day he/she scratched a nose.

(13) Grandma often grabs daddy/mommy by the scruff of the neck when they scold, march them down memory lane and remind them they too terrorized the dog, pouted, leapt from roof tops, ate incessantly and were sometimes taken in front of the mirror to admire a purple tongue after munching on a ballpoint pen. Parents often forget their own sins. It's up to grandma to refresh their memory.

(14) Strangers are not interested in seeing home movies and slide presentations starring a complete cast of grandchildren; nor is it necessary for Grandpa to become owly when he discovers Grandma has contracted to have a perfectly good house re-sided by a door-to-door salesman who seemed to enjoy the show.

Each of our grandchildren have a distinct personality; each is a rare human being and each continues to have the ability to send Grandma and Grandpa scurrying to a vacation resort that sports a large sign saying..."Absolutely No Children Allowed."

We wouldn't have it any other way.

"ONLY CHILD FINDS LIFE DULL"

Finally we have a child who has fulfilled her destiny. She is an "Only Child." Older brothers and sisters are on their own. She is a sibling without a "sible." No longer does she have to wear left-overs. No more torn pockets and mismatched mittens. She can put stereo headphones over her ears without the fear of having earphones (and ears) ripped off by an aggressive older sister sneaking up behind her. She's the only one needing hot lunch money and scheduled for the SAT test.

She can squirm at the dinner table and not start a chain reaction. She has a certain proprietary air toward the telephone...and her father.

"Only Child" was very pleasant when it all began. So was I. After all, it was a brand new experience for both of us. For years, I'd been conditioned to think in multiples. I viewed cooking as tonnage rather than tasteful. I didn't sort laundry...I shuffled it around. A red shirt went into the soapsuds with a pair of navy blue socks. So be it. She eventually wore them without complaint. It was expected of her.

"I've worn nothing but purple for years," she sighed pleasantly, turning up her nose at a murky mauve nightgown. "It will be so much fun to wear yellow and bright blue and scarlet." The two of us stood arm-in-arm beside the washing machine admiring the small assortment in the clothes hamper and the fact that it no longer bulged and overflowed.

"These are my very own shoes," she squealed in delight. "And this is my very own room with my very own bed and my very own bulletin board and my very own electric blanket. And Augie is my very own dog!"

Augie's ears stood straight up. He felt he could certainly benefit from having single love lavished on him. For years he'd been pummeled and pushed in many directions...often having to choose between treking off with the boys on a golf ball hunt in a nearby creek or staying home with the girls to be dressed as a doggie bride-groom so that he could marry the cat. It would be a pleasant change for him to know where he stood. He followed "Only Child" about the house like a furry shadow.

"Everytime I turn around Augie is there," "Only Child" complained." So is Daddy."

"Give them time to adjust," I soothed. "They will soon get used to quiet halls and silent rooms. I certainly have." And I quickly crossed my fingers behind my back in case Someone Up There was listening and might suspect I was telling a little white lie.

Unfortunately, I found that "Only Child" was a doubtful household helper. "Please run the vacuum in the living room," I asked nicely.

"Grumble, grouch, growl," cried "Only Child."

"Will you get a loaf of bread from the freezer?"

"Snarl, snap, snip," was "Only Child's" answer.

"Run to the store and pick up some lettuce."

Threats, thunder, tears was the response.

"Why do you always pick on me?" she sobbed.

"Because you are it. Because you are an "Only Child".

The bloom was beginning to fade.

It was obvious to anyone who cared to notice that fingerprints on the window were definitely hers. She couldn't palm them off on a sister who was no longer there. A stolen lick on a newly frosted cake belonged to only one tongue. And it wasn't her brother's. If a door slammed I knew instantly who slammed it. A dish dropped on the floor, broken into a hundred pieces and tucked tidily in the garbage can beneath a newspaper, held no mystery. I knew immediately who tucked it there. The safety of the family line-up had suddenly disappeared. I needed no witnesses to the crime. She wasn't even given the benefit of a fair trial.

"I get blamed for everything," she accused.

"Who else is there? You are an "Only Child.""

She grieved that popcorn didn't taste half as good when it was popped and munched all alone. Trying her best to get Augie to fight over who got the "old maids" failed miserably. Fighting over popcorn was beneath a dog's dignity. He only fought over good things like moldy balogna or an occasional cricket.

There wasn't a soul in the house who appreciated MTV or backed her up when she wanted to spend $20 on tickets to a Rock Concert. She was a minority of one and often the parental communications system was lousy. "You don't understand!" she cried out and no one answered "Amen".

Long distance telephone charges began to show up on our bill. They covered two states. Now my husband hadn't made these calls, I hadn't and I was sure, despite his basic intelligence, Augie hadn't made them. It had to be "Only Child."

"Why?" I asked.

"Because I'm lonely," she said. "I wish they'd all come home."

And do you know something? Sometimes I do too.

"WHEN THEY ARE ADULTS - THEY WON'T FIGHT - HA HA!"

Possibly the only brothers and sisters in the world who don't bicker and brawl on occasion are, in reality, paper dolls or little Hummel figurines. Certainly no flesh and blood child of my acquaintance ever passed up the opportunity to snarl in a sister's direction when mom wasn't looking and it seemed only natural for a brother to reach across Augie Doggie's furry nose to slug the jaw on the next pillow if an elbow or knee jerked in just the wrong manner.

When they were toddlers their methods were quite unsophisticated. A brother would carefully wind up the battery on a motorized yellow Corvette and let it race over his sister's head, resulting in hysterics and a quick haircut. Lincoln logs were a major source of ammunition and nothing strengthens a child's first set of teeth like sinking them into the unsuspecting shoulder of someone who is stealing a favorite cuddly rabbit. In order to survive four older sisters and two bigger brothers our youngest child bit her way through the first three years of her life. She was as quick as a German Shepherd and to this day has earned the upmost respect of family members. All she had to do is draw back her upper lip and everyone gives in to her.

This doesn't mean I approved of their quarreling. Heavens no. If given a chance to choose between being stuffed in a closet with a big black grizzley or spending a day with seven cross children I'd take my chances with that old bear any day. At least it would be a quick kill. More than once my husband returned home from work to find me huddled in a nervous heap on the couch.

"The children fought all day," I moaned.

"Ignore them," he suggested. Easy for him. He was 30 minutes away from the battlefield. I was stationed on the front lines. "Daddy's home!" was the cue to wave the white flag.

Not that they really drew a lot of blood. In fact, as they grew older, the girls seldom touched flesh. Theirs was of the "talking tongue" variety of combat. Often I wished they'd get the whole thing over with in one hearty punch instead of rattling the walls with words.

"That's my shirt!" a sister screamed at another. "You are wearing my shirt." Down the stairs she clattered.

"You took my shoes yesterday," came the rebuttal. "If you can take my shoes, I can take your shirt." Up the stairs she went with arms banging the bannisters.

"Take your old shoes. Who wants them anyway. They make my feet smell." A door slammed.

"Your hair smells. I need some air. Gag...gag!" A window is thrust open.

"Your's is stringy." a chair is kicked.

"Stop!" I cried out. "Why do you have to fight so much? You are sisters. Can't you share? Can't you be friends?"

"With her?" The vanity, six dresser drawers and a row of encyclopedias were piled up to form a Berlin Wall down the middle of the bedroom they shared. .

"Never!" And the tears flew through the atmosphere like spring raindrops. By the time my husband came home I was exhausted from playing Little Mommy Peacemaker and told him he'd better settle those girls down if he didn't want me to have a terrible headache for a whole week.

"What do you mean 'Settle them down'?" he asked."I just peeked into their room to say hello and they were trying on each others clothes and complimenting hairdos."

Our sons, on the other hand seldom used words. Quietly and without fanfare they simply pummeled each other like play dough. Juvenile muscles squirted juices like grapefruit as they backed each other into a corner and silently squeezed each other into submission. I suppose if Augie hadn't tipped me off by barking loudly they would've eventually ground each other into dust.

Augie hated watching the children fight as much as I did. He liked them all (much as I did) and couldn't choose a winner. His doggie conscience wouldn't let him pitch in and help the loser. My mother's conscience wouldn't let me help either. About the only thing left for the two of us to do was to yelp and hop up and down. Evidence of their conflict came in torn shirt pockets, broken knick-knacks and once in awhile, a fat lip.

I worried they would grow up hating each other. My husband reassured me this wouldn't happen. "When they are adults, they won't fight...you'll see." And he was right.

Recently our oldest son was asked to be Godfather for a little niece. He loved the title and felt he'd finally reached his destiny, strutting through the house much like Marlon Brando, mumbling incoherently and looking at himself in the mirror. After the new wore off and we were no longer expected to drop to our knees and kiss his ring when asking for small favors, I turned to our youngest son and asked...."Why him?"

"Because he's my brother, mom," he said.

And I guess that tells it all.

"A RESOLUTION FOR THE LIMBS"

I will be giving up something new and different this next year. It is something that, in the past, I have enjoyed and taken some pleasure in. No, it is not eating! Nor is it smoking, speaking or sex.

It is a personal thing...something that will effect no one but me...and my feet. I am giving up escalators. The reason is simple. One tried to kill me.

"That's silly," said my husband. "You know and I know that escalators do not purposely try to maim people."

"Then why," I ask, "did this one deliberately chew my foot?"

"It did not chew your foot?"

"It did"

"It didn't." Now, this could go on forever and ever and no one would win but the escalator and it has already claimed one body...it need not win anymore prizes.

I have always assumed that escalators were very safe. They either went straight up or straight down without deviation and they do not move too fast. I realize they aren't colorful but then neither am I. I felt as if I was embraced in the footwork of a trusted friend when I stepped on an escalator to go from floor-to-floor. I loved looking out over the sales racks as we passed slowly by better dresses. I could spot a $20 mark-down from the 10th step.

But that is all over. Escalators are no longer a part of my life. They have now entered the list with airplanes, elevators, and horses. If God intended for us to fly He would have given us a jet stream; if He intended for us to go reeling or plummeting, He would have furnished cables in our armpits. If He had intended for us to gallop we would all have four legs and if He intended for us to move gently from one floor to another in large department stores He would have fastened rollers to our feet...therefore I am not going to mess with the unknown. From now on it is strictly walking if I want to get anywhere.

"Don't expect me to walk with you" my husband said. I didn't. "Besides" he repeated, "It really wasn't the escalator's fault. Admit it. You just weren't looking."

He is right I suppose. I suppose if I had been paying attention I might still have a good relationship with escalators. Nevertheless, I am entering the new year with a busted knee and a bruised ego. And despite any excuse my husband can offer, the escalator did play a big part in it. After all, it did spit me out on the floor for everyone to see and laugh at.

I wasn't wearing spike heels or a tight skirt when I stepped on-to the escalator. I was wearing workaday shoes and a rumpled pantsuit. I have to admit that it was tight...but it was safe. I boldly planted one foot before me, as I have seen fashion models do on television, and we made our slow ascent upward. Everything was definitely under control.

"Look, look," I told my husband as we passed from first floor to second.

"Can you see the crowd pressing over by expensive colognes. There must be a clearance sale. Don't let me forget to stop by there on our way out of the store. Better still, don't you forget to stop there on your way out of the store."

"Watch what you are doing!" he said, turning me forcibly around by the elbow so that I, again, faced the front. "You are go-ing to fall," He was overreacting. We had hardly advanced. A long stretch of moving steps lay before me.

"Look, look," I tempted our daughter. "There is a fuzzy, white sweater over there in the corner that would look just right on you." I craned my neck to see if I could see the price tag.

"Good heavens, mom, pay attention!" she shouted moving down to blend in with another family whose mother stood like a stiff soldier, eyes pointed in one direction.

I glanced ahead. We were half-way up the steps. I wondered why they were all fussing so. There were so many things to see. So many bright and expensive things.

"Look, look", I turned to touch our grandson. "See the funny big bear." A large blue teddy bear grinned from a perch between floors. Our grandson's little eyes tried to focus on the big bear grandma was talking about. He wanted to please grandma. He knows which side his bread is buttered on, but all he could see were the tops of people's heads.

"There, there!" I said directing him with pointed finger.

And that is when the escalator struck. Like poetry in motion I reached a horizontal position from a perpendicular one. That escalator squirted me out as simply as someone squeezing an orange. I was stretched unceremoniously on the floor of a crowd-ed department store.

Our grandson giggled and clapped his hands. The bear he couldn't see. Me-he could.

Forcefully and with a mighty heave, daughter and husband each took an arm and boosted me back to my feet. We entered the mainstream of customer traffic...me limping, my daughter trying to appear she was a good Samaritan assisting a stranger, our grandson bouncing up and down gleefully and my husband laughing out loud.

Well, I can tell you this, if they are going to have murderous man-eaters in department stores, the least they could do is provide rescue measures. They could put someone at the top and bottom to administer mouth-to-mouth resuscitation if necessary.

And if they would choose Robert Redford to do this, I might reconsider my New Year's resolution...well, wouldn't you!

"CUPID HITS THE JACKPOT"

"Hi, Little Cupid."

"Hi, Lady."

"Next week's the big day."

"So they tell me."

"Aren't you excited? I am. This is the year I could get that diamond necklace."

"More than likely it will be a bouquet of dead daisies."

"Why would you say a thing like that?"

"Because I've been watching and your husband hasn't smiled in two weeks."

"I'd rather not talk about it."

"Headaches are back, huh?"

"Shame on you. It has nothing to do with headaches. He's a little upset that's all."

"Why is he upset?"

"Why should I tell you?"

"Because if you don't I'm going to shoot you in the ankle with my bow and arrow."

"You wouldn't."

"Try me."

"Since you put it that way. . he's upset because he said I made a perfectly awful scene in public."

"I thought it might be something like that."

"It really wasn't a 'scene'. . just a misunderstanding. We were in Las Vegas, see," and I'd never been there before and I wasn't sure I even wanted to go but then I read in our fun book that Wayne Newton would be there and I told my husband I'd be glad to go if I could see Wayne Newton."

"Why would anyone travel that far just to see Wayne

Newton?"

"You'd have to be a grandmother to understand."

"Did you gamble?"

"I'd rather not talk about it."

"Did you win?"

"I'd rather not talk about that either."

"Every cupid I've ever talked to that is stationed in the casino areas swear they have earned enough chips to retire any time they want. They say EVERYONE wins in Las Vegas."

"Sniff. . Sniff. . that's what I thought."

"Hey, lady, don't cry."

"I had a terrible time, Little Cupid. Pretty girls in short, short skirts kept coming around and saying 'Want a drink, ma'am?' and I didn't know if it was morning, noon or night because I couldn't find a clock and my husband was pulling at my elbow and yelling in my ear... 'You can't drink before lunch...you'll get sick' and I told him it wasn't polite to ignore them and besides I needed something to hold my nickles and if I didn't empty the glass the money would've sloshed around and gotten all slippery."

"Oh boy, I get the picture. No wonder your husband hasn't smiled. You got smashed!"

"I did not!"

"What happened then?"

"I got my arm...mumble...mumble...mumble."

"Speak up...I can't hear you."

"I GOT MY ARM CAUGHT IN THE SLOT MACHINE."

"You don't have to shout."

"And you don't have to laugh."

"How in the world did you get your arm caught in a slot machine?"

"It ate my nickle."

"And you went after it...that figures."

"You can't imagine. It was a horrible experience. Bells were ringing and sirens clanged and the machine kept flashing "Tilt" and some elderly gentleman threatened to hit me because he said. I was ruining his favorite machine and an old lady with a shopping bag full of nickles accused me of cheating and the hotel owner came down and said he'd never had this happen before and if everyone would go and mind their own business he'd take care of it."

"Where was your husband?"

"It's funny you should ask that. The hotel owner asked the same thing only he talked out of the side of his mouth and walked on the balls of his feet. I told him my husband was right over there and then I looked and he was gone and I didn't see him again for three hours. And I didn't have any more nickles, my arm was all bruised and I never did get to see Wayne Newton."

"Did your husband win anything?"

"He wouldn't tell me but I noticed when we got home he borrowed four dollars from our son to pay the paper boy."

"Well, you know what they say, old girl. Lucky in love...unlucky...etc. etc. etc."

"If you don't mind...I'd rather not talk about it."

"FANTASIZING ABOUT LEAP YEAR DATES"

I can remember when I was a teenager in the unliberated 40's and Leap Year meant that I could legitimately ask the captain of the basketball team for a date. Of course, he refused but this didn't keep me from repeating the invitation every 15 minutes.

He eventually reached the point where he was so nervous from avoiding me in the school corridors, he fouled out four games in a row. The coach blamed it on poor nutrition, his mother blamed it on the coach and the head cheerleader blamed it on all those evenings spent in the back seat of his Chevy convertible. Only the basketball captain and I knew the real reason.

My husband, who is a wise and sometimes nervous man, patiently explained that Leap Year actually had no romantic connections at all. He told me it is a year in which a 29th day is added to February to compensate for the difference between the length of the common and astronomical years.

"Each year," he droned on, "divisible by four is a Leap Year, except those completing a century, which must be divisible by 400." I was so confused my head ached.

"Blame it on Julius Caesar," he continued. "He put the extra day on the calendar about 2,000 years ago." I wondered if Mr. Caesar wanted a date with a basketball captain, too. My husband grinned and said probably not because he was far too busy with Cleopatra. For a minute there, he looked envious.

I hate it when someone takes all the juice out of a tradition and reduces it to dusty scientific facts. I liked it ever so much better when I could spice up Leap Year with a few frills and a bit of fantasy. Naturally, I've outgrown high school basketball captains but this doesn't mean I can't dream.

Let's take Larry Bird for instance. A professional basketball player, he has nice blonde hair and quick hands. When he dunks, slams and stuffs, he nearly takes my breath away. I think he'd make a perfect whirlwind date for Leap Year. He might not appreciate short and dumpy so I'd have to wear some very high heels. I estimate about 12 inches. Think about it. I'd be tall all right but wobbly. I suppose he'd bring along his gym bag. Well, that does it. I've washed the contents of enough gym bags to squash any erotic notions I might have about Mr. Basketball Bird. Sweat and stink is sweat and stink. I don't care who it is.

Prince Charles is out. He'd expect me to wear a hat, sip tea and have a baby every two years. I did that with my own prince but at least I didn't have to do it in public. I'd hate to have a Queen for a mother-in-law. What do you want to bet she doesn't babysit or ask everyone to come to her house for Sunday dinner.

It ran through my mind I might consider George Burns as a prospective date for Leap Year. We're probably the closest in age but he IS getting up there and before I'd chance going out with him, I'd want to update my mouth-to-mouth skills in case of emergency. But then I don't particularly like cigars and the thought of tap dancing for three solid hours bores me to death.

Burt Reynolds wouldn't be a bad choice but I think Dolly Parton has him all sewed up. I can't compete with Dolly. Not many of us can.

"As long as you're being silly, why don't you set your trap for the President of the United States," my husband said. "You've always claimed you were destined for the White House until you got sidetracked in Nebraska."

I could probably handle the President. He's a nice man and nearly as old as George Burns. Come to think of it, living in the White House might be a kick. At least their silverware matches and when the children come to visit, no one would have to sleep on the floor. Then I thought about the fact the wife of a President is expected to have her hair combed at all times and she's never, never allowed to answer the door barefoot. That's a lot of pressure to put on a person.

I suppose I could take a shot at Johnny Carson. Everyone else does. Do you think Ed McMahon would expect to go with us everywhere we went? That wouldn't be much fun. And I'd hate ironing all of Johnny's shirts. I'd also hate to face up to the fact he has more clothes than I do. Looks better in them, too. I like

Johnny a lot, but he keeps irregular hours and probably has a late dinner. I have indigestion if I eat more than two peanuts after 8 p.m. It's doubtful he'd appreciate a love affair with someone who swigged Maalox instead of martinis. So much for Johnny.

Robert Redford is out of the question. I'd faint in five seconds if he so much touched my fingernails. What good would it do me to date Robert Redford if I was unconsious for the rest of my life. I feel much the same way about Paul Newman, Andy Williams and the Fuller Brush Man.

I was running out of choices for my big date on Feb. 29th. I had one more.

He was sleeping in his big chair with his chin on his chest, his glasses gently resting on his mouth and his newspaper on the floor. I recognized him right away. He is the one that laughs hysterically when I cry along with my best soap opera friend, Marlena; the one that thinks popcorn is gourmet; the one that's shrinking right along with me so that soon we'll be the same size and when he dunks, slams and stuffs, it's his doughnut in a cup of coffee.

On the other hand, I'm grateful he doesn't tap dance.

I'd have to go a long way to find someone that I like as much as I do him. Let's face it. I'm not Cleopatra either but sometimes he's kind enough to act as if I might be.

You can't ask for a better Leap Year date than that. Now can you?

"NUTS TO THE SQUIRRELS"

There was no one in this world happier to see February end than I was. If we can make it through March there's a strong possibility we will see flowers bloom again. Well, not in our yard but the neighbors are bound to have a few nice tulips and things.

"Why don't butterflies ever come to your house, grandma?" our granddaughter asked last summer. We were surrounded by gnats, moths, large flies and inchworms...there wasn't a pretty butterfly in sight. "They come to ours, sometimes," she added.

I explained to her that Augie-doggie didn't stand around in her yard and click his teeth at everything with colorful wings. "The butterflies are afraid of Augie," I told her. "They are afraid of grandpa, too." She looked quite surprised at this. She couldn't understand why anyone would be afraid of her kindly, old grandpa. But then he'd never roared around chasing her with a spray can of DDT either. I've seen bright yellow butterflies turn pure white when they saw my husband turn the corner of the house.

But as ferocious as Augie and my husband might appear to butterflies they don't scare the squirrels that have invaded our area this past winter. A fearless and brave band of furry soldiers, our neighborhood squirrels continue to thumb their noses at dog and man as they go about the business of trying to eke out a living. Much like the rest of us they've had a long, tough, cold winter.

"Poor little buggers," I told my husband. "How can they find nuts to eat when there isn't a nut tree within miles of here. Don't you think it would be nice if we could buy them some?"

"I'm not paying $2.50 a pound for nuts to feed squirrels. I bought them corn. What more could they ask for?"

"Oh, they snarfed that up hours ago," I told him. And indeed they had. Scrambling and scratching for the last bite they reminded me of our sons, home for a holiday dinner. I fully expected to have one or two peck on the door, ask for a cold beer, hint that I do their laundry and then stretch out on the ground for a post luncheon nap while I cleaned up the leftovers.

In bushy tailed eagerness they are there when I get up in the morning to put on the coffee, peering in the kitchen window to see what I am preparing for breakfast, hoping against hope, it will be something good and squirrel edible like scrambled acorns and hot, black walnut cakes.

"Hate to disappoint you, kids," I said as I cut a grapefruit in half. A hefty fellow splatted his body to our window like a decal. "Look," I said to my husband. "he has tears in his eyes. Can't I give him some of our breakfast?"

"Squirrels don't eat grapefruit!" my husband hooted.

"They might," I said and I placed a large rind on the back step. Immediately Mr. Hefty called his wife and the two of them pounced down and carrying the grapefruit between them like a suitcase, they scurried up to their nest. Mrs. Hefty was back in a split second, hoping I suppose, that I'd slip a bit of sugar in a saucer to sweeten her husband's breakfast.

Declaring he'd have no more to do with strange squirrels, that ate grapefruit for heavens sake, my husband shook his head and went out to fill the birdfeeder with sunflower seeds. "You can count on birds to eat what they're suppose to eat," he said and sat and waited for the cardinals, blue jays and sparrows to fly in.

Guess who came to dinner! It was as if we'd blown the noon whistle. Squirrels lined up for a block and Mr. and Mrs. Hefty brought their entire family, including second cousins to have a go at those sunflower seeds.

My husband stood beneath the tree with Augie, hoping at least one squirrel would loose its grip and fall on its head. "Growl , Augie," he snarled. Augie growled and Mr. Hefty flipped a seed in his right eye.

"Put your feet on the trunk of the tree and bark." Augie did as he was told and an affectionate Mrs. Hefty ran down and kissed him on the ear. "I'll get my shotgun," my husband shouted and Augie went in to lay under the kitchen table. He wanted nothing to do with mass murder...even if it was squirrels. I reminded my husband it was against the law to fire inside the city limits and asked him how he'd feel if someone took a pot shot at him while he was trying to eat. He mumbled something about having more pride than to eat birdseed and sat down to read the paper.

A continuous queue of squirrels filed down throughout the afternoon, dining scrumptiously from the birdfeeder. By nightfall it was empty and they stood outside our house, chattering for more. "Poor mites," I said sadly, "They are still hungry. What will we feed them tomorrow? We have no more corn...no more birdseed."

"Too bad," my husband said, hardening his heart and his purse strings. "Let them work for their food like I do. We'll say no more about squirrels," and as far as he was concerned the subject was closed tight and so was the little squirrel's breadline.

But I needn't have worried. The next morning I looked out to find **three perfectly cut and trimmed grapefruit** sitting on our back step. A spoon full of sugar was nearby. I knew right away I hadn't put them there. I wonder who did!

"GIRL SCOUT COOKIES TASTE BETTER THAN EVER"

Possibly we are the only family home in America who will soon have a freezer full of Girl Scout cookies instead of T-bones. I can never resist a Brownie Scout when she knocks at my door. And, quite frankly, I think the news has spread. I think our house is marked with a magic symbol that says "Stop here...this lady buys cookies and buys cookies and buys cookies."

We've had these wee super salespersons come from as far away as South Dakota, but that's O.K. because that particular Brownie was a granddaughter and everyone knows the real heavy spenders at cookie time are grandparents. They buy dozens and dozens of boxes even though they are on a strict diet, are not allowed to eat sugar and haven't touched a cookie for seven years.

Grandparents are soft touches when it comes to Brownie Scouts. So are Brownie Fathers. But the very special person in this miniature scouting world is the Brownie Mother and the Girl Scout organization will happily accept this mother if she can do two things...breathe and drive a car.

X-ray eyes were not necessarily a requirement but they were nice to have. As a Brownie Mother I was expected to be able to spot the beanie in the bottom of the toy box at 70 paces one minute before the school bus was due.

I was also expected to whip up steaming dishes of beef stroganoff, au gratin potatoes, baked beans, a "different kind of jello salad, mommy, one with whipped cream" and at least two devil food cakes for a Father-Daughter banquet scheduled for six p.m. And one that I knew nothing about at 4:30 that very same afternoon. Father didn't know about it either but all he had to do was put on a clean shirt, smile and be sure and bring home our good silverware.

As a Brownie Mother I was obligated to take my hitch at Day Camp. I would've enjoyed this more had I been 18 years old, weighed 98 pounds and wasn't allergic to wood ticks. As it turned out, when camp rolled around, I was usually suffering from post-partum blues or I was eight months pregnant. I also had arthritis, two broken toes, a migraine and my hair was stringy.

It was very difficult for me to hold back a definite snarl when my neighbor insisted she couldn't go to day camp because she had a cold sore and didn't want to be seen in public. "Next year," she promised. "I'll go for sure. It's so much fun I hate to miss it. You all have a good time now, you hear," and she stood in her doorway and waved as I grumbled down the road in my green kneesocks with a co-op cap pulled down over my ears.

During the five days...the five very lo-o-o-o-ng days of day camp, I woke at night in a cold sweat and tried desperately to erase the nightmare of being gobbled by mosquitoes. In my sleep I tossed, turned and shouted, "Who ripped off the Caper-Chart?" causing my husband to bolt out of bed in fear of being mistaken for the latrine and suddenly finding himself disinfected to death.

When my own personal Brownie ordered six cases (instead of six boxes) of Savannahs I dutifully paid for them and proceeded to serve them for breakfast, bridge club and important dinner parties. I tried palming them off on the PTA but they weren't having any because the teachers already had some. In fact, they had a lot.

The teacher of a second grade Brownie is in a worse spot then a grandmother. She either buys from every Brownie in her classroom and is labeled "precious but poor" or refuses to buy from anyone and is called "rotten and rich."

Often I was forced to make a size six uniform fit a size 12 body so she would look proper for her investiture.

"She looks stuffed into that dress," a brother critically observed as he pulled into the driveway on his bike. I was taking a snapshot of this very important day. The Brownie was posed before a lilac bush and until that particular moment seemed quite pleased with herself.

"Go away," I hissed and soothing hurt feelings I told her she looked just like all the other little girls in her troop. And she did. It wasn't until years later, when she came upon the picture in the family album, that she admitted to nearly strangling in that tighter-than-tight dress. I asked her why she hadn't complained. "You were so proud of me," she said. "I didn't want to ruin your day."

And I was proud. Proud that she tried to live up to the Brownie promise by being kind to others. "Does that mean HIM, mommy?" and she pointed to her brother. I assured her brothers were people like everyone else, and yes, it included him.

Everytime I take a bite out of one of our millions of Girl Scout cookies my memories go back to the days when I, too, was a Brownie Mother. And the older I get...the sweeter each bite becomes.

"SEXY LADIE'S"

Lives there a husband in this world who doesn't stand before the window display of a smart little lingerie boutique and sigh wistfully at that which he views within. My husband is no exception.

"Wow!" he said. "That's the kind of stuff you should have," pointing to a cobwebby creation in black.

"In the middle of March?" I replied. "Good grief, I'd freeze to death. It's much too cold outside for me to wear that sort of thing inside."

"But you were saying just the other day that you needed a new nightgown, didn't get one for your birthday and look, the store is having a big sale. It says five percent off...boy, you can't do any better than that."

"Oh, yes I can," I said primly. Naturally I wanted to make my husband happy, most wives do, but not at the expense of waking up in the morning and discovering I had turned into a large, lumpy ice cube.

I explained to him that I would be willing to wear the tiny nightie if he would be willing to flip the thermostat up to 85 while we slept.

"You know I can't do that," and he was shocked that I'd even suggest it. "The President of the United States would probably hold me personally responsible for the energy shortage if I did anything like that. I don't want it on my conscience."

I suppose he was right. But I wanted to please him. "A black flannel granny gown with a little lace at the sleeves and the throat would do it," I thought. "That would take care of his illusions and my body heat." I set out that very day to buy one. I searched every store within a radius of 100 miles and suffered the humiliation of being laughed at by every salesclerk in every store I entered.

"There's no such thing as a black flannel nightgown," one of the salesladies cackled hysterically. "People who go to bed in black definitely aren't the flannelette type."

"Well, I am" I said stiffly, turning on my heels and walking right out of the door with my head held high. "I'll show that silly salesclerk. I'll just whip that baby out on my sewing machine. Who knows I might start a whole new trend in nightwear. Surely, there are other ladies out there who would wear black flannel."

My husband said he doubted it very much.

Once again I started my rounds of the stores, avoiding the

lingerie departments and the snooty eyes of their salesclerks, concentrating on yard goods. I found pink, pale green, light blue, printed and checkered flannel but no one seemed to have any black. "I only need a few yards," I begged.

"But I've never had anyone ask for it before," a poor confused clerk said. "Why do you want it?"

I didn't make the mistake of telling her. I simply lied and said I wanted to make curtains for my husbands darkroom. I thought it was a brillant answer and was quite proud of my quick mind.

She seemed to believe me and suggested corduroy instead. "I do have some cheap black cord over here on a bolt."

I couldn't see sleeping in corduroy so I dropped my head sadly and told her my husband was very allergic to it as well as cotton, knitted goods, all polyesters, wool and satin.

"Flannel is the only thing I can use," I said. I'm sure she wanted to ask me if he wore a flannelette suit and tie to work but was kind enough not to. She accepted my word, sighed and said that the only thing she could suggest was to dye the material. I thought that was a very good idea so I bought five yards of white flannel and a box of black dye.

I was proud and anxious to get started.

"See what I have," I showed my husband. "A magic box that will give us both what we've dreamed of..your wish and my warmth." And with that I shoved material and black powder in the automatic washer, turning the machine and the hot water on full blast, and let her rip. Soon I had a black washing machine, black utility room floor, black fingernails and a black cat that was once stone white. I also had black flannel, I pointed out, when my husband complained that I had certainly made a mess. "Now all I have to do is sew it up."

"I can hardly wait," my husband said.

It took less than two days. I worked hard and when I finished I had a voluptuous coal black granny gown with delicate lace outlining the top and the bottom. For a racy touch I added a huge red Velveteen rose at the throat.

My husband laughed right out loud as I got ready for bed. I didn't expect that kind of a reaction. He said I looked like a yawning witch. I don't think that was a very romantic attitude, do you?

It was unusually warm in our room when I awoke the next morning. In fact, I think you could truthfully say it was hot! The red rose drooped, the lace was wilted and permanently engraved on our best, most expensive percale sheets was a large black spot. "My gosh, I faded on the bed," I shouted. "My new nightgown is ruined. So are the sheets. Who turned up the thermostat to 92?"

My husband admitted that he had. He also admitted that he'd rather take his chances with the President of the United States any day than sleep with a black flannel witch.

I can't say that I blame him.

"AN ICY MIDNIGHT RIDE"

My husband claims I'm the only person he knows who hasn't minded this winter's cold weather because I'm the only person he knows who still sweats when it's ten below zero. "I don't know how you do it," he shivered as I danced across the kitchen in a gossamer nightgown. "I'd think you'd turn into a block of ice." He was wearing a flannel robe, woolen socks and had a stocking cap pulled down over his ears because he'd read somewhere that most of our body heat escaped through our head.

He's wrong. I do mind it. I'm no different than anyone else. It bothers me to see icicles draping our picture window instead of curtains and it gives me a creepy feeling when snow sifts in under the door. I get no kick out of tossing a howling Tippy-cat outside when I catch her eyeing the flower pot in the corner of the room and I can hardly bear the tears on Augie's furry checks when I explain to him that it looks silly for a dog to stand in the middle of the living room floor with four paws crossed and that he might as well accept the fact he is going to have to go out that front door sooner or later. "We all have to, fellow," I told him.

And I am very, very tired of walking around town like a penquin.

"Mark my words," I said to my husband as I minced along beside him clutching his arm so I wouldn't slip on the icy sidewalk. "After this winter generations of children are going to grow up walking like little elfs. They will know no better. Each step I take measures no more than three inches." Oh, how I yearned to break out in a long, free, yard-wide stride. I hadn't walked naturally in six weeks. I was certain that eventually there would be permanent damage to my leg muscles.

"If you'd wear decent shoes," my husband hissed. "You wouldn't have this problem."

"I'm not wearing army boots with a velveteen dress," I hissed back, as my left ankle went right and my right ankle went left and I flopped unceremoniously against his hipbone.

"You'll end up maiming us both," and he braced himself against a light pole to keep from falling to the ground. As we leaned there I thought for a moment we might stay there...just the two of us...immortalized forever as plump snowmen.

But I have to admit, walking beats skiing down the highway in an LTD. It isn't much fun driving sideways on the interstate...especially when I was huddled in the backseat, our son was at the wheel and my husband was sitting in the passenger seat and I watched as the hair on the back of his neck slowly rose out of sheer terror.

It has always been my policy not to drive with our two sons or our son-in-law under the sunniest conditions...and knowing I was going to be at the mercy of our oldest son with icy patterns on the road precipitated shortness of breath and red blotches on my forehead.

"Young persons have better reflexes," my husband rationalized as he handed the keys to our son.

"Why don't we stay where we are?" I asked. We were in a strange city, 145 miles from home and parked in front of what was probably the local bawdy house...but I didn't care. Self-preservation was more important than morals at this point.

"I can't stay overnight," our son whinned. "I have a date and besides I don't have a toothbrush."

"A toothbrush will not make one iota of difference if you don't have any teeth," I snarled, visualizing the car heaped in a snowbank, our collective molars scattered alongside like kernels of corn.

"It's not that bad, mom," our son said and it really wasn't. It was only after we reached the point of no return that it became hazardous. A giant iceberg, with Kitty Clover written on the side, rolled by and I prayed the driver could handle that semi skillfully. I would hate to think I would be snuffed out by a potato chip. By now, my husband's hair was standing straight up and as it has happened before, bits and pieces of my life flashed before me.

"It's still dull," I sighed. But things were picking up as the car did a slippery buck and wing in the middle of the road.

"I've got it! I've got it!" our son screamed. Obviously he didn't have it and I thought my husband's hair was going right out the window and I was huddled in a tight little ball with my head between my legs to keep from fainting dead away and adding a bit more excitement to a trip that had already raised my blood pressure to the sky.

"It's O.K.! It's O.K." our son continued to screech as we happily went laterally down the road." "We're nearly home!" And as we pulled into the driveway he turned to me and said "I wasn't scared." Why then, was his lower lip bitten into? "I wasn't scared either," my husband whispered trying to smooth down his wild hair.

Well, I was! And I said so... out loud.

But when you get right down to it...all of the snow we've been having in Nebraska does have its good points. It's been a notable way for God to hide some of His worst mistakes. Even our garbage cans look nice in their little white hats.

"LOVE, MRS. LUETH"

I received a letter recently from an old and valued friend. Well, she's not o-l-d, not that kind of old, she's younger than I am. This, however, does not classify her as "spring chicken." But then again, she's not o-l-d. She was the principal of one of the elementary schools our children flitted in and out of a few years ago.

We became close out of association and desperation. I had the most children enrolled in the school and she was responsible for keeping track of them. Neither of us had an easy job.

In the letter, old (There's that word again) and valued friend reminded me of something which I remember as the "Chicken Caper." It involved the first grade teacher, our first grader and a chicken.

This wise first grade teacher knew that the three, perfectly darling, baby chicks being used as a "teaching experience" would soon grow into three, perfectly ugly, big chickens unfit for ANY kind of experience so a lottery was planned. They were to be given away to the lucky child whose name was drawn from the pot. But, first, mother had to give her permission.

It was well-known by me that when student names were drawn for May King and Queen, Captain of the kick-ball team and "the one who gets to raise the flag," our children's names disappeared from the drawing. But let them give away a lizzard, 10 gold fish, white mice or the stray, school kitten, our name popped out of the hat like magic.

I knew this. This is why I refused to sign anything that came from the school. I was even reluctant about some report cards but then that's another story. But I wouldn't sign for the chicken. I thought the matter was closed. I had underestimated our child's resourcefulness.

A letter appeared at school. It went like this:

YES, WE CAN HAVE A CHICKEN ANYTIME. LOVE MRS. LUETH.

I did not write this letter. The teacher knew this at once. The "love, Mrs. Lueth" apparently gave it away. Our child had been driven to forgery by my refusal to accept that silly chicken. I was beginning to look like a bad mother.

I explained to the teacher there were at least three good reasons why the poor chicken would be taking its feathers in its hands if it came to live at our house...they included:

(1) Augie, Nancy and Dolly (dog, cat and cat) had enormous appetites and were not above eating other animals smaller than they were.

(2) The father of the household also had an enormous appetite and was not above eating animals smaller than he was...especially fond of chicken.

(3) The mother of the household had a very bad disposition along about 5 p.m. while preparing dinner and was not above striking anything that moved...chicken included.

I hastened to add that if she still felt the chicken would find a secure and peaceful home with us and if she wanted very much to get rid of it, she could send it home with our child.

We didn't get the chicken. Our next-door neighbor did. She was an only child and led a protected and quiet life. She often dropped by our house to zip up her day and increase her vocabulary.

One day chicken came with her. Our dog ate it. Right there. Feathers and all. Chicken was gone. I was the only one that cared.

Next-door neighbor didn't care. She had grown rather tired of following it around with a rag. Her mother was elated. And until he chewed up that poor chicken, her mother had hated our dog. They became the best of friends. She even petted him when he tromped through her strawberries.

I suppose, if it's a chicken, some good even comes from murder.

"THE CANDYLAND CHAMPION"

Faced with being left at Grandma's house for the first time in her innocent life without the security of her mommy's lap and her daddy's strong shoulders, Laura Elizabeth showed signs of real concern. She was being thrown a curve and the look on her sweet face was one of quiet desperation. It wasn't that she didn't like Grandma and Grandpa. She did. She came into our house happily, toting 95 percent of her possessions and settling in without a care. We received hugs on arrival and sad tears on departure.

She was obviously content as long as she could reach out and touch the people who allowed her to eat pizza for breakfast. Being in the same house...alone...with the lady who hawked yucky cereal as more suitable fare was a different matter.

She had to be prepared for such trauma. Her parents started two weeks in advance. For fourteen days they painted pretty mind pictures of what fun it would be to spend time at grandma's house. They promised everything but a personal visit from He-man. And Grandpa and Grandma were instructed to let her win at Candyland.

"Why?" Grandpa asked. Grandpa doesn't like to lose at anything.

"Because," our son explained. "the book says children should be allowed to win at games until they are seven years of age."

"We didn't do it like that," my husband reminded him.

"I know," our son shuffled his feet. "I remember."

So did I. If anyone was allowed to win in our family it was Grandpa. It worked out better that way for everyone. Drawing our son aside, I assured him that we'd cross that bridge when we came to it. "I'm sure I can arrange her winning," I told him. "Haven't I done it for years for your father."

It wasn't like Laura Elizabeth was going to be left at our house forever. It only involved a few hours. I couldn't understand her reluctance. Our own children were always happy to see their parents leave. I used to worry about it. Now that I look back, maybe it was because, at last, they'd have a decent chance to be a winner.

Taking Laura by the hand, her mother showed her the clock. "See," she said. "When the big hand gets here and the little hand there, we'll be back. Grandma is a nice lady. She will give you cookies."

Laura Elizabeth looked disappointed. She'd eaten some of Grandma's cookies during the Christmas holidays. She knew they weren't worth the sacrifice.

Sitting down beside his tiny daughter, our son entered into a long, detailed psychological explanation of why it was often necssary for parents to leave their little children. "It's good for everyone concerned," he said seriously. "Everyone needs their own 'space' in this world...even parents."

Bored to death, Laura kicked pointed shoes against my best coffee table and tossed her golden curls.

"Just go!" I ordered.

"You mean just walk out!" Our son looked startled and I thought his wife would faint dead away at such an awesome suggestion.

"I mean...just go!"

"She'll cry."

"That's a distinct possibility."

"We can't stand to see her cry," they said in unison.

"It will only last a few minutes. Trust me. I know what I'm doing." Silently, I pledged to give them three more minutes of sputtering and then I was going to throw them bodily into the yard.

Putting on warm gloves, our daughter-in-law gave me a desperate look and asked if I'd make her poor baby eat awful things.

"She can eat anything she wants," I sighed. "Including Augie's dog food."

Removing her gloves, our daughter-in-law balked. "I'm not going," she said quickly.

"Mom was only kidding," our son said. "She won't let her eat dog food. She'd never let me and God only knows I tried often enough. Sometimes Augie's dinner looked better than ours."

"Just go!" I repeated for the third time.

Reluctantly, the two of them edged toward the front door, hoping I'm sure that Laura Elizabeth would immediately throw a fit so they would have an excuse not to leave her in the hands of a woman who was obviously a bad witch in an apron and baggy jeans.

However, at that particular time, Laura was engaged in a desperate battle in Candyland. She was winning the game...fair and square...and Grandpa's face was a bright pink. She crossed the finish line as their car left the driveway.

Realizing they were no longer in the house, she got up from her chair, walked to the door and turned the lock as firmly as she could. Brushing her hands together she said, "Well, that's THAT for them!" and resigned to spending the remainder of her life with the odd old couple she returned to thrashing her Grandpa at Candyland.

After being beaten for the fifth time Grandpa softly unlocked the door when Laura Elizabeth wasn't looking.

"SPRING BRINGS NEW BEGINNINGS"

I will tell you one thing...if Mother nature doesn't get her dust pan and broom out pretty soon our house could very well be the first to be burrowed under stray sticks, dried leaves, brown, unidentifiable crunchies and a dozen or so left-over Augie-Doggie bones. Obviously, our yard needs a good Spring Cleaning. So does our house. And I suppose, so does my soul.

Following the Easter season I always want to push wintertime back into the dusty windows of my mind. I want to bring out the spray mist and wash away all of the picayune, piddling insults and small frustrations that I've let accumulate and chill over the months of cold winds and snow. Unlike most people I make my New Year's resolutions in April.

"I will not," I told myself, "nag my husband about the chuck holes in the driveway!" and revving up the motor of our car I flew backwards into the street, knowing that if I slowed down to look I might be bogged in forever. I knew, too, that if I didn't drive straight I would come in direct contact with a very large and very hard oak tree. I'd never really hit this tree square-on before but I'd come close enough to reach out and shake its leaves as I skimmed by. I blamed it on potholes and my husband blamed it on pure ignorance.

"I'd never noticed it before," he said in amazement as he stood on the porch and watched as I rumbled the ignition key and prepared to drive into town, "But the car shivers when you drive." I remembered my resolution and bit my tongue. He will eventually get the driveway fixed just as he will eventually paint the garage, mend the bird-bath and find new lids for our garbage cans. My job is to sit back, keep my mouth shut and wait patiently for these things to happen spontaneously.

"Don't take it personally," our daughter-in-law said when I walked happily over to Laura Elizabeth to pick her up and was greeted with a scream of terror that nearly tore my left ear off. "The book says that seventeen month-old babies always react that way to strangers."

"But I'm not a stranger," I puckered. "I'm her grandmother."

"She'll get used to you, mom," our son said. "Take it easy and give her time." I gave her an entire weekend. She continued to cringe and tremble every time I entered the same room, I took off my glasses and her eyes widened in fright when I put my face next to hers. I tried not speaking, thinking perhaps my loud voice was the trigger and went about silent and sad, tiptoeing up behind her to give her a kiss on the back of the head. She cooed in cuddly, contentment until she turned around and saw who had given her the kiss. I thought she was going to faint.

"My God," I cried, "she hates me!" And I watched this poor frightened baby have a classic case of infant hysterics and as her mother and father tried to soothe her I tried to melt into the wallpaper and become invisible.

"She doesn't hate you," my husband said. "She's only people-shy. Babies are like that you know."

My babies weren't. They were so friendly with strangers it was all I could do to keep them from packing their diaper bags and going home with anyone who happened to drop in. Now here I was causing little Laura Elizabeth to draw back in horror and dig her fingernails into her mother's face every time I made a sudden move.

"Well, I'll just go sit in the bathroom until it's time to go home," I pouted. It certainly doesn't take a brick wall to fall on me to let me know when I'm not wanted. The thought that I was singlehandedly turning my very own granddaughter into a spooked little kid nearly broke my heart.

"Look at it this way, mom," our son soothed. "She'll learn soon enough which side her bread is buttered on. I did." And he reassured me that they would place my picture by her crib and each night chant "Grandma! Grandma! See the nice Grandma! Grandma buys toys and candy and brings pretty dresses to good little girls."

I tried to pretend that this satisfied me.

I also closed my eyes and tried to remember when I was a young parent and our children were small and as our two-year old grandchild ate a brand new box of crayons and her brother opened the oven door, gagged and said "What's dead, grandma?" I recalled how I'd reacted when my very own children did the same thing. And I guess I decided that somewhere along the way I'd forgotten how to scold and learned to smile instead and that's the nicest thing about Spring...she, too, forgets to scold with icy winds and smiles instead with warm breezes.

To me, Easter has always been the official declaration of spring and I noticed that last week my husband had moved the paint cans outside, put some cement by the driveway and bought new lids for the gargage cans. Our son called with the news that Laura Elizabeth was climbing and the first thing she headed for was my picture. No one got sick when they ate crayons or the supper-in-the-oven and with my usual optimism I say...."Happy Spring!"

It's a brand new beginning!!

"RESCUING THE FAMILY CHICKEN"

I remember the Easter I saved a life.

I did not receive any outstanding recognition for this feat...I did not get my name and picture in the newspaper. The President of the United States did not call me long distance, person-to-person, to congratulate me.

The only one that was tickled about the whole thing was the chicken. The chicken was really glad!

You see, it was the chicken I saved. A little yellow chicken, named "Fluffer." It lived in our guest room-in our house. To go into WHY it lived in our guest room in our house and not outside in a regular chicken place like any normal chicken is much too complicated and no one would believe me anyway.

It had something to do with the fact the three younger girls wedged themselves under my feet, turned sullen and sobbing threatened not to eat, drink their milk or sleep. I thought about this awhile, weighed all the circumstances and decided I did not want this type of situation discussed in the teacher's lounge at school and gave in. The chicken was allowed to live in our house.

We had no real idea if this was a boy chicken or a girl chicken. I rather thought it was a boy chicken since it was periodically grumpy when its food dish was empty. On the other hand, it chirped a lot and my husband felt this indicated definite feminine qualities.

There was much conversation over the dinner table concerning the sex of this chicken. The younger children soon began to lose faith in their father and mother because we could not pin down the necessary facts needed to establish the proper name. Was it "Mr. Fluffer" or "Mrs. Fluffer?" No one knew. And I didn't really care. Neither did my husband. He was really losing interest in that chicken...fast. And he was gaining quite a bit of interest in me..and the fact I had allowed the chicken to live in the house.

The teen-age children had followed the whole conversation with deep attention.

One or two had a few choice comments to make and one was sent from the table without dessert.

The chicken actually lived well, considering its neutered state. It had a split level house. Made of cardboard boxes. With curtains and a bedspread. It had a bedroom, kitchen, toy room and living room. Unfortunately, it did not have a bathroom.

The children forgot this one little item during construction. Possibly they did not understand the mechanics of chicken plumbing. I don't know. I do know the nonexistence of this particular room caused more discussion, by my husband at the dinner table than its unknown sex.

Perhaps, if the chicken had had its own bathroom, in its very own house, it would not have wandered into our bathroom and into its feather-raising adventure.

Technically, it was not supposed to be allowed out of its own spacious living quarters. In reality, when someone left the door to the guest room open, it streaked out into the rest of the house like a roadrunner...chirping and flapping its wings. This was the part my husband had developed such a deep interest in.

And this lack of discipline nearly caused the chicken to streak its way into heaven.

It went for a swim-in our bathroom-in the stool. And it couldn't swim.

But, boy, could it tread water!

By the time I found it...screaming...its legs were out straight and stiff...propelling like crazy. Its feathers had lost the dry look. It could definitely be described as slick...like it had been dipped in salve. Its eyes were popped and I could see clear down to its tonsils.

That was one scared little chicken!

A quick scoop of my hand, a wrap in a soft towel and chicken was safe and sound. It was exhausted, poor thing, and immediately fell asleep in its upstairs bedroom...with only an occasional gurgle.

The thought uppermost in that little chick's mind while it was treading for its life MUST have been "Don't flush... please, don't anybody flush!"

"NO ONE WILL EVER CONFESS"

A deep mystery to parents is how to solve the problem of "Who's to Blame?"

It's easy enough when you walk into a room and the kid has meringue on his upper lip. He's the one who took the slice out of the lemon pie.

At our house, however, I always found the pie had disappeared but everyone had clean lips. When I curled both fists into the air and yelled "Okay, who ate the pie?" our oldest son swore he hadn't had a bite of food for two days.

"I'm starving," he said quietly, "but I'd never ever touch your pie, dear mama." Obviously he'd folded his angel wings beneath his T-shirt. I couldn't see them but surely they were there.

"I'm on a diet," a teenaged daughter confided. "I don't eat sweets." I wondered to myself who was putting the candy wrappers in her dresser drawer. I didn't say anything. I didn't want to be the one responsible for warping her tender mind.

"I'd never do that without permission," another angelic voice whispered. She was practically flying through the air with pure innocence.

"I bet a tramp came in the back door and got it" our youngest child said seriously. "They do that on television." I didn't even bother explaining that in this day and age, tramps no longer snitch pies but prefer stereos, silverware and strong boxes.

My husband claims trying to discover the blame is the hardest part of being a parent. "No one will ever confess." he sighed. "If just once someone would stand right up, look me in the eye and say 'I did it, dad', I'd go to my grave happy. What did George Washington's father have that I don't have?"

A wig, fancy farm and a potential president I told him.

Our children have outnumbered us for years. Once we were equal. Once we had two little girls and two big parents. Even then it was hard. Oh, it worked out swell when one was 14 months old and the other two weeks. We knew right away the tiny infant in the bassinet hadn't jumped up and dumped over the potted plant. But our toddler gave it the old college try. She set the mold. She gave 'passing the buck' a dirty name.

"Baby did it," she said sincerely when I asked my first silly mother's question..."Who made this mess?" I think she actually believed it.

As pre-schooler's they had no qualms about placing the blame on someone else. "Augie pooped in my pants," our three-year-old son came to me one day walking funny and with a surprised look on his face. "Bad doggie."

"Mary Poppins was here dusting and broke this vase, mommy," our little daughter said primly. Isn't that awful!"

As they outgrow bizarre alibies they moved to flesh and blood realistic ones. Each other. "It had to be her," a brother pointed to a sister. "I was 3,000 miles away when daddy's electric razor blew up."

"Don't look at me," our daughter said when I showed her my brand new expensive lipstick snapped at the stem. She turned to her brother. "He's the one who will eat anything."

Gradually, however, as they became older they formed a strong coalition. Not only did they stop admitting to personal crimes, they wouldn't squeal on each other. If a fight broke out in the playroom...no one started it. According to them, it happened by osmosis. The grunts, small slaps and stomping feet could reach a fevered pitch but let me ask who was to blame for the fight and calm settled like a warm blanket.

"We're not fighting," a son gasped between chipped teeth. "We were only playing." He threw a friendly arm around his brother's bruised shoulders and limping away together they looked back to see if I was still watching. If I was in sight, they smiled and held hands. If not..grunts, small slaps and stomping feet echoed down the hallway.

Once in awhile, though, I demanded justice be served. Such was the case of the mysterious disappearance of the PTA Easter Doughnuts.

That year, when straws were drawn during the previous meeting of our PTA, I had lost the drawing, and "volunteered" to chair the school's annual spring Easter Tea. Two other mothers were appointed to serve with me. We were the committee. "We might be small...but we're mighty," I promised as I bowed among the handclaps of the relieved members who had won the draw. "We'll have a grand tea this year."

According to one on the committee she worked 24 hours a day away from home and the other had migraines. "I'll do what I can to help during my coffee break," the working mommy said tiredly.

"If I can open my eyes for five minutes without fainting, you can count on me to fold napkins," the other offered in an aching voice. Together they said "You aren't busy. You do it."

It wasn't really that hard. I simply ordered ten dozen yellow and green frosted doughnuts and asked if they could be sprinkled with bright glittering stars. "No problem," the baker said and had them ready days in advance of the tea. I picked them up from the bakery and they were beautiful. Placing the three long boxes in the freezer I called the school principal to tell her everything was under control. "I'm glad," she said. "This is our last event of the school year. It's important things go smoothly."

Did they go smoothly? Or did a tramp come and steal them all? Read on and find out.

"A MYSTERY SOLVED"

The morning I reached into the freezer and found eight of the ten dozen pretty doughnuts purchased by the PTA and pledged to the PTA...g-o-n-e; all g-o-n-e, I lost my cool. How was I going to explain to the other two committee members that I'd lost the doughnuts? How could I admit to the school principal I'd botched her annual spring Easter tea? Suicide seemed to be the only answer.

I could replace them of course, but these doughnuts had been special; lovingly decorated with tiny glittering stars sprinkled among the glaze. The minute I showed up with the less expensive substitutes everyone would know I'd failed the PTA. Again.

Furious at the gaping space where the prized doughnuts had once rested I ran up the stairs shouting "EVERYONE IN THIS HOUSE GET UP THIS VERY MINUTE!"

Bodies flew out of the rooms, some sobbing from fear, some grappling for decent clothing in case there was a fire, others grumbling and one or two trying desperately to find where they'd stashed their angel wings the night before. They figured they were going to need them.

It was a terrible jolt for my husband to discover that his wife had gone completely and possibly irreversibly beserk during the night.

Augie, who had headed straight under our son's bed the minute he heard footsteps on the stairs, was so confused he was barking and snipping his teeth at lint.

"You, too, dog," I yelled, hauling him from beneath the bed and sending him with a soft smack on the furry behind down the steps.

Lining everyone up in front of the dining room table, I suspected the guilty ones because of the shocky film that covered their eyes. They might as well have had a doughnut hanging from their noses. I knew who they were but went through the maternal motions of a fair trial.

"On your honor," I commanded. "Who took the doughnuts?"

"I didn't eat the little doughnuts," our youngest child trembled.

"Not me," our oldest son claimed.

"It wasn't me," another daughter chimed in.

Our high school junior reminded me that she was on a diet and certainly wouldn't eat eight dozen doughnuts. "I haven't tasted anything sweeter than lettuce for six weeks," she sighed.

"Don't blame me," my husband yawned. "Can I go back to bed now?"

The real crooks tucked their chins so far down into their pajama fronts they all but disappeared. It was our fifth, third and first graders. All three had their eyes shut tight so they wouldn't see the horrible sight of their mother exploding in the middle of the dining room.

"It was Augie's idea," our ten-year-old son explained. "He thought it up." Augie looked stunned.

"Now, I don't believe that," I said. "Try again."

"It was her fault," and he pointed to the third grader.

"She did it," the third grader motioned toward the first grader, who seemed as stunned as Augie. She was only six years old and here she was being accused of masterminding a doughnut snitch. At that moment, I'm sure she didn't consider life very fair.

"He told me to," she said, putting the blame where she thought it belonged. Now, we were back at the beginning of the trio. I was getting nowhere.

"You will all have to sit on the couch and stay there for the next twenty years or until someone tells the truth," I said. "Remember, twenty years is a long, long time."

"It's not like it's for the rest of your life, kid," our oldest son grinned at his brother. "Just the good part."

Eventually, I learned what had happened to the starry doughnuts. A small impromptu neighborhood party had been conducted one Saturday afternoon while their dad was acting as chief babysitter.

"There were a lot of kids at our house, mommy," the first grader said. "We had fun."

"The doughnuts were frozen but no one cared," our son admitted.

"Daddy made the Kool-aid before he took his nap. We were really quiet." The third grader smiled gently at her father, who, by now, was wide awake with a sheepish look on his face.

"I wondered why things went so well that day," he said shaking his head.

It was up to me to gather up enough courage to call the school principal and tell her we might be serving baloney sandwiches for the school Easter tea. It took me two hours and when I picked up the telephone I still hadn't ruled out blaming the whole thing on a tramp.

The principal laughed for ten minutes. For all I know...she's still laughing.

"Remember," she told me, between giggles, "The youngsters at the party are all from our PTA anyway...the doughnuts went into the correct stomachs. Easter just came a little early this year, that's all."

I was so relieved that she had taken it so well that I decided not to bother the other two committee members. I'd just let them be surprised.

We did have doughnuts for our tea. They weren't pretty starred ones, however, just plain, and three of the school children at the party refused to eat even one. They said they never wanted to see another doughnut again as long as they lived.

I, on the other hand, had nine.

They tasted swell.

"MOTHERS LIKE TO HEAR
'GOOD NEWS' "

Recently our family sat around the dinner table and as I looked each of them over carefully, I stiffened my spine and prepared to give them one of mother's little lectures. I often do this to keep them on their toes and to let them know I still love them. "When I stop telling you what to do," I once warned, "That's when you'd better start worrying."

My husband said they'd better not get their hopes up.

"I have only one complaint," I confided, removing a piece of buttered bread from my hair where Laura Elizabeth had so thoughtfully placed it. "For months now not one of you has called home with good news. Last week I had four collect telephone calls...Someone had lost their contacts; someone said their checking account was zero; someone had been laid off and someone wanted to know if I knew a good lawyer. What is a mother to do? Doesn't anything pleasant ever happen?"

In unison they raised their heads from the table and said "Not often!" Now I can hardly believe each hour of their lives is a bummer. They were all brought up with the maternal philosophy that once in awhile the bear gets you and once in awhile you get the bear...Why then, don't they ever share with me the times when they triumph over the bear !

"It's simple, mother" a college daughter said. "If I call and say I have a date with a nice boy you have me wed, moved into a large split-level and you've started a little pink or blue sweater set. I don't dare tell you the good stuff."

"And mom," her older brother seconded. "If I tell you I've gotten a raise you remind me of the $20 I borrowed from you five years ago to go to Colorado to see the Rolling Stones." And I'll keep reminding you I said quietly under my breath. Loans for the Stones aren't considered charity in my mother's book.

Another daughter giggled and said each time she told me of the "A" our granddaughter received on her report card I'd contacted the State Board of Education and invited them to make up an engraved plaque with her name on it to present to her school, "I told them I'd pay for it," I said primly. "I simply can't understand their attitude when they hung up on me."

And I couldn't understand our children either and turning to our daughter-in-law who still treated me with respect I pleaded with her to tell me something pleasant that had happened in the past week or so. "And I'll expect each of you to think of at least one thing," I warned.

"Well," our daughter-in-law said, "Laura Elizabeth learned to dance." (Talk to someone in charge of the television show "Fame" and see if they need an 18-month-old genius ballet princess.)

"I really did have a date with a very nice boy" our daughter admitted shyly. (Order announcements, check real estate ads and stock up on pink and blue yarn.)

Our son took a deep breath and whispered that his employer had complimented him on the terrific job he'd been doing. "I've nearly reached my quota for sales," he said proudly. (Find out if politics is a paying proposition and investigate where the-mother-of-an-American-President is listed in the encyclopedia.)

"Your grandson can count to 20," his mother said happily. (Where is the-grandmother-of-an American-President listed?)

During this entire mass confessional one of our children remained very, very quiet. A professional student, she was one of our major bearers of bad news. According to this particular daughter, her life was as tangled as a ball of twine and as the others strained to come up with something cheerful she sat with bent head and a secret in her heart. Finally she could stand it no longer...

"I have something good to say," she said quietly.

"Wonderful!" I clapped my hands. Everyone else looked up with startled eyes. Even Laura Elizabeth stopped making puddles with her chocolate milk. It seemed our family Typhoid Mary, who carried bad news like a disease, had something positive to contribute. It was a real red letter day, indeed, and we all waited breathlessly for her to continue.

"I won a competition," she said. (Miss America Pageant? Phi Beta Kappa Key? Graduate School Rhoades Scholarship?) "I'm going to represent the University in a regional pool tournament."

I didn't even know she was into swimming.

"Not as 'In swimming,' mother," she corrected me. "But as in 8-ball."

Her father said "Good for you!" and her two brothers and brother-in-law seemed impressed and somewhat envious. However, I was quite stunned. For some odd reason I'd been under the impression she was going to be a teacher instead of a feminine Minnesota Fats. That just shows you how dumb a mother can be.

"It's sponsored by the Student Union," she explained, "And I'll be going with the chess, backgammon, darts, bowling and checker teams. There will be nine women and 30 men."

"Wow! Listen to those odds," a younger sister sighed. "Do you need someone to carry your pool cue? I'll volunteer." This was exceptional news in itself as this child seldom volunteered for any thing that didn't include $6.50 per hour plus fringe benefits.

"Will there be a chaperone?" I asked.

"College students don't have chaperones," she said firmly. Somehow I seemed to be missing out on the "good" portion of this entire conversation. My husband pointed out later as she advanced to the national competition, if and when she seeks employment any school in the nation that requires a female elementary classroom teacher with snooker skills our daughter is a shoo-in for the position. I suppose I'd consider that good news...wouldn't you?

"A WIFE IS BETTER THAN BAIT"

My husband is so enthusiastic about fishing that he often loses sight of the fact he married a bimbo that prefers curling up in a warm corner to sitting on a frosty bank with wet feet and a damp fanny. Two weeks ago he came home, eyes sparkling, rubbing his hands in anticipation and said "I heard the crappie are biting at the lake."

"Terrific," I shot right back. "Let them bite. I won't bother them if they won't bother me." Tired and cross because of an early frost warning, I'd spent hours carrying in the outside plants because of the nip in the air, taking them back outside because they needed sunshine and then bringing them back in because they started shivering. All morning long I'd shuffled those plants in and out...in and out. The geraniums had lost their blossoms and the Bosten Fern had turned into fourteen thousand bare strings all tangled up in one pretty pot. I'd worried those poor plants into an early grave and now my husband wanted to do the same thing to me. "It's much too cold to go fishing," I told him.

"Nonsense," he cried. "It's hot in the sun!" and he stuck out his arm so I could feel how warm his bare skin was. The goosebumps were so high I could've hung towels on them and the tip of his nose had a light blue cast. "It will be invigorating to spend an afternoon in the fresh air. And we could catch our dinner you know," he said, grinning like a man who'd been invited to Camelot for a light supper and a go at a vestal virgin.

It isn't that I'm against fishing. I'm not. Ordinarily, I go along with him happily because I've worked out a nice system that includes taking along a comfortable chair, two good books, a sackful of treats, cold and/or hot drinks, wash cloth (in case a worm touches me), a small portable television and a transistor radio. When I pack the car, my husband usually mutters something like "if I'd known you were moving I would've called Mayflower" but because he feels taking half the household is better than listening to me whine he doesn't say too much. All in all...we get along well.

Until two weeks ago...when he decided economically we should find our own bait. "We'll just dip a few minnows out of the river and be all set," he explained. Now everyone knows it is practically impossible to dip anything out of a river that is rolling like a soccer ball, tumbling with great brown muddy waves and colder than the Artic Ocean in February. I could swear I saw an iceberg peeking up north of the bridge.

"It's your imagination," my husband said, as he stepped into the water, trying hard not to faint when the icy waves hit his shins. "You'll have to carry the minnow pail while I net." He handed me an orange bucket, said don't drop it for goodness sake, told me to follow him and keep as quiet as a mouse.

I learned an awful lot that afternoon. I learned that if you didn't wear elastic-waisted jeans up around your neck they had an embarassing tendency to slip down around your knees while wading in hostile water; that minnows have a lookout that warns the rest of their family to go and hide the minute someone steps into the water with a net and bucket; that my husband turns ugly when I inadvertantly scattered an entire school of minnows as I threshed about and cried "I'm in quick sand. Help me...help me!" And that the clock stands still when a person is doing something they hate.

It took about an hour to collect two dozen elusive minnows. I was freezing to death and could no longer feel my toes and my husband promised...one more big sweep and we'd be done.

This made me happy and I gave a tiny skip of merriment. A major mistake. As I skipped the strong tide pulled at my hips, caught me off balance and started sucking me into the water. I had two options...I could throw the minnow bucket up into the air and save myself or keep the bucket at an even level and let ME sink into the river. One look at my husband and there was very little doubt which of us he considered indispensable. I could read his mind..."Pooh-a wife," he seemed to say, "I can get one of those any old day...but a batch of bait takes skill."

Naturally I rescued the bucket...I bet you knew I would...and sitting down squarely in the middle of the Platte River, I was soaked up to my armpits. With chattering teeth I called out..."The minnows are all right!" For a split second I thought he was going to haul in his net, wade to shore and leave me there all winter. But, remember, I had his bait! A wife he could possibly do without but if he wanted to fish he needed that bait. Therefore he reluctantly came to help me up. I wouldn't give him the bucket until he did. I'm no fool.

"I suppose," my husband sighed, "We'll have to drive all the way home for dry clothes and by the time we get back to the lake the minnows will have suffocated and the fish won't bite." He looked oh, so sad.

"Never mind," I told him and reaching back into my stash of stuff in the back seat I produced a sack full of dry clothing for both of us. As I said...I'm no fool. "I always come prepared," I smiled. "Let's go fishing, Tiger."

And for one day...for one moment...I proved to the world (and my husband) that a good wife is more important for a successful fishing trip than bait.

"OPEN LETTER TO JUNE BRIDES"

I suppose you really don't have time to read this. If you've already had your wedding you're either on your honeymoon or still in shock. If the wedding is coming up I bet you haven't looked at any type of reading material but a checklist in weeks. Perhaps your mother-in-law will clip this out and save it for you.

Please know that I don't pretend to be an expert on marriage. Heavens no. Simply because I've been married for 32 years doesn't make me expert...tired maybe, but not expert. And you must remember that I don't know your husband as well as you do and actually, I don't really want to. I have enough trouble with the one I have without taking on strangers.

But in many ways they are all alike and these little hints won't do any harm. If they don't work for you, pitch them out with the garbage.

And speaking of garbage, there will be a few times when your husband might accuse you of throwing away perfectly good foodstuffs, household items and important mail. Don't over react but allow him to take it back out of the garbage, dust it off and put it away. The next day you can toss it again but this time wrap it carefully in something HE has discarded or hide it in a tin can, empty detergent box or shred it so thoroughly it's unrecognizable and then bury it quietly in the middle of the contents of your garbage can.

Don't expect him to help you write thank-you notes, letters to his family or Christmas cards. For some unexplainable reason most men lose complete control of their writing techniques the minute they take a wife.

They will be most happy to have you sign your name to everything but personal checks and credit card applications and quite often you might be asked to sign something without reading it. And you probably will because you have faith. But let me warn you that in the upcoming years it is quite possible that you will endorse white slavery (yours); co-sign a loan to buy dryland property to be used as a duck blind; make yourself available for an immediate jail sentence by area IRS agents. When he says "Sign here honey, you don't have to bother your little head with this old dull stuff," don't be blatantly suspicious but try to peek at the fine print if you can.

Money almost always plays an important part in any marriage. I bet you knew that already. It will be the topic of many bedtime conservations as well as breakfast, lunch and dinner.

You will probably discuss the following items...(1) The spending of money...(2) The lack of money...and (3) Who gets what? For some reason, unknown to God and most women, he will mention several times your paying $12.95 for a pair of scissors that will last a lifetime and then turn around and spend the same amount on a cottage cheese carton of nightcrawlers that dry up and die in fifteen minutes.

If you could possible sneak into his home before marriage and clean his closet of old shirts he's had since Junior High, baseball caps that are so dirty they hang on the walls without pegs and cowboy boots that have the original cowpie plastered to the bottom you will be well ahead of the game and are apt to have nice closets. Otherwise you'll fight these same objects for the rest of your married life and no matter how hard and how often you wash and scour, they will never come clean or disappear. And your mother-in-law will NOT take them back. Come to think of it, she probably won't take your husband back either.

You can, in all fairness, point out the fact that you are still using your great-great-grandmother's treadle sewing machine when he brings home an expensive riding lawn mower to cut grass on a plot of land that measures 12 ft. by 18 ft. But don't dwell on it. I warn you right now, if you nag about lawn care too much you could find yourself mowing, roto-tilling, clumping earth, fertilizing, replanting, trimming and fighting ugly crawly creatures for the next 45 years or more.

And never, never admit that you know how to use a screwdriver, change a light bulb or wield a paint brush because if you do-your middle name might well become Mama Maintenance. The first time I was asked to help with a home project I hit my husband's thumb with the hammer and he's never asked me to help again. Of course, there for a short instant our entire marriage was touch-and-go.

If and when you do an interior decorating gig together let him be "Management" and you be "Labor." In that way you can always go on strike for fringe benefits and sometimes the fringe benefits are the very best part of being married. Trust me.

But I wouldn't choose to hang wallpaper together. Mercy no! It definitely won't glue a marriage. I'm not going into detail and describe the husband-wife scenario of hanging wallpaper together. It's pretty X-rated and not fit for a family book. Perhaps some day when I feel brave..I'll tell you.

And then will come the first time you say to him.."Darling, I think we are expecting.." if he says "WHAT?"...don't tell him.

He deserves to be surprised!

"OPEN LETTER TO JUNE BRIDEGROOMS"

My husband demanded equal time after reading about the June brides. And because I believe in being fair I gave him the opportunity to talk back. He said he'd really rather take the time to play golf but if I insisted he'd jot down a few things about women that might come in handy for any poor altar-bound sucker that might want to read them. I asked him what he expected in return and he said invitations to every bachelor party in the area for the next five years. I reminded him that he'd hardly survived our son's bachelor party so how could he expect to handle them in dozens and he said he thought he could manage. This only goes to show he still has a few surprises left up his wrinkled sleeves.

And speaking of surprises...new brides are full of them. As far as that goes, so are old, worn out and broken down brides. Nothing jolts a fellow quite so much as the sight of his beautiful lady emerging from the bridal bathroom in a set of curlers. Where once blonde, flowing locks grew, now sprouting from this sweet head is an accumulation of appliances wadded up on top of her head like a cable company. "If I'd wanted to marry barbed wire," Bridegroom mutters, "I would've married 'Ranch and Valley, Inc.'."

Twenty minutes after the honeymoon starts, she not only discards her flimsy nightie for an oversized football jersey with an old boyfriend's number on it..but smells like a wet chicken.

"But your scent was so seductive when we dated," Bridegroom sniffles, trying hard to recall when his new wife reeked of roses rather than roosters. According to my husband, this is only the beginning. In the next few decades the Little Wife will give off odors of pot roast, pickle juice and poopy diapers. Bridegroom might as well get used to it.

Despite the fact things were quite agreeable before marriage, Mr. Bridegroom, don't expect this to continue. When once she showed a great admiration for your prowess as a mighty hunter and provider of fresh meat she will now look upon you as an animal killer. As long as your mother cleaned the game things were in their proper prospective. Now that she is expected to do it you might as well steel yourself to heavy lectures on humanitarianism, assassination and showing mercy to every creature in the woods. And don't expect her to cook it or eat it without tears in her eyes and great sobs and gags.

Be ready for the evening you come home from work and find her sitting in the living room in the dark, her head hanging clear to her knees. This is called "Guess What Is Wrong With Me!" She isn't going to give you a clue so you might as well save yourself the bother of asking. You'll have to probe. Here are sample suggestions to start with...(1) She has left your nifty and valuable little sports car in a ditch somewhere. (2) She has just received a telephone call saying your application to bowl on the town's championship team twice a week has been accepted. (3) She wants to go out for dinner.

Number three is probably something you should do at least once a week anyway just to keep on the safe side.

Accept the possibility that she is going to go through your pockets. Women are insatiably curious. However, if you ever approach her purse, be prepared to have your hand snapped off at the wrist. A woman's purse is more valuable than her virginity. You can have her body, but leave that pocketbook alone!

Household projects will probably consist of her buying the paint and you doing the work. Oh, she will have marvelous plans, possibly to the point of purchasing several chic outfits to go with all the new wall colors but when it comes right down to the actual labor she might whine, struggle and admit ignorance of which side of the paint brush to use. She'll praise your natural talent for such a craft and then stand over your shoulder and shout if you drop one glob on the woodwork.

Your best defense is to tell her you have always wanted to live in a house with dirty walls and as a child dreamt of peeling ceilings. Women are maternal pushovers for husbands who speak of their childhood. Tell her your mother was a crone and kid, you have it made. That is, you have it made until your mother finds out!

Your new wife will, in all probability, be spiritually warm, somewhat sophisticated and sweet-as-pie when you hand over your paycheck. She will worry about you, fuss over you, coo in your ear and then demand that you kill every mouse in the house or she will divorce you on the spot.

It will remain a deep dark mystery to you how someone, who so outspokedly and determindly loved and cherished every little critter on four legs can get so excited and upset about a simple mouse. Guaranteed, if one enters your house and she sees it...brother...you'd better get busy. There are a lot of things a person can't (or won't) concentrate on when she thinks she hears squeaking under the bed. Take it from a pro!

Eventually of course, your wife will become a mother. This makes you a father. And a whole new set of rules go into effect. A few basics remain, however, and they include Forgive...Forget...and Keep Your Mouth Shut.

If you do the above and do it in good spirit and with a smile on your face you'll receive many Father's Day presents and perhaps get to attend as many bachelor parties as you want.

"A CONVERSATION WITH LAURA ELIZABETH"

"Hello, grandma," a little girl answered the telephone. It was the voice of a tiny angel.

"Hello, Laura Elizabeth," I said back. "What are you doing?"

"Oh, me painting me toenails and me legs green," she said.

"Grandma loves you," I said quietly.

"Me come to your house. Daddy said."

"Put Daddy on the telephone, sweetheart."

"Daddy on the couch."

"Tell him to get up right this minute and come talk to his mother."

"Daddy not here."

"Where is he now, honey?"

"Him went into the bathroom and locked the door."

"Go knock."

"He said 'Go away, little girl'."

"Knock harder. Like you really mean it."

"What do you want, mom?" our son's voice sounded strained and very tired.

"Laura Elizabeth said you were coming to visit. I just wanted to know when so I could warn the cat. And your father."

"It will be soon," he sighed. "Very soon."

In the silence, someone, sounding suspiciously like our daughter-in-law, said "Go ahead and ask her. You said you would."

"Do you know what it's like living with a two-year-old Queen?" our son blurted out.

Actually, I did. Hadn't I lived with five Queens, two Princes a big King and one Sir Dog for years. I wondered why our son couldn't handle one tiny angel.

"What's the problem?" I was certainly enjoying myself.

"She says...'me want...me want...me want'. Do they ever stop saying...'me want?'"

"Yes...yes, they do," I promised. I could hear our son's relief for 150 miles. "Soon she will say 'I want'. Two year old's often outgrow baby talk by the time they are three."

"That's not what I wanted to hear," our son said. "The Queen wants to talk to you again."

"Hello, Laura Elizabeth. What are you doing?"

"Me sing to Mickey Mouse." And she did. For ten minutes.

"That's nice. Let me talk to daddy."

"Him went back to the bathroom."

"Go knock again."

"What now, mom?" our son asked when he reluctantly returned to the telephone.

"I'm only trying to help. Why don't you take her for a walk?"

"We've walked fourteen miles since sun-up. It isn't even noon. I can't go another step."

"Have her take a nap."

"Are you kidding?"

"Take her to town and buy her a new toy. That's what I do."

"She stands in the middle of the store with tears running down her face and begs...'Two, daddy, please...two!' It costs me a fortune."

"I know," I told him. "I know."

"Guess who wants to talk to you."

"Hello, Laura Elizabeth. "What are you doing?"

"Me cry."

"Why are you crying, my darling?"

"Me wants my mittens."

"Honey, you don't need mittens. It's April."

"ME WANTS MY MITTENS."

"Go knock, sweetheart. Grandma wants to talk to Daddy."

"This could cause some real medical problems, mom," our son growled."

"Calm down and tell me why Laura wants her mittens on such a nice April day."

"She's eating pizza."

"What does that have to do with mittens? You don't need mittens to eat pizza."

"The Queen does. She doesn't want to get her fingers icky."

"So what's the big deal. Give her the mittens. You're not in public."

"But we might be. And she never forgets. She'll do it in public. I know she will." There was a long pause as a small angel voice and a deep growly voice argued in the background. Several 'me wants' and one loud' Here's your dumb mittens' drifted over the wire.

"Hello, grandma."

"Hello, Laura Elizabeth. What are you doing?"

"Packing me little suitcase."

"Why?"

"Me come to your house. Daddy said."

"But grandma will be in the bathroom for the next three or four weeks I'm afraid."

"That okay. Daddy said all me had to do was knock."

"WHAT DOES ROBERT REDFORD HAVE THAT OLD DAD DOESN'T HAVE?"

With Father's Day approaching I sat down the other day and compared my husband and subsequently my children's father with Robert Redford......

"What does Robert Redford have that Daddy doesn't have?" our youngest daughter asked.

I clutched my heart.

"The same thing that Dolly Parton has that your mother doesn't have," I answered. I was being honest, realistic and sad.

But you can't keep a person from daydreaming. Not lusting, mind you, just simple daydreaming. I wondered out loud the other day what it would be like if Robert Redford really would drop in on Father's Day. I could picture him riding his Electric Horse right into the driveway. I bet he doesn't even sweat.

"You'd just yell at him, mom," our son commented. "You'd scream 'hang up your coat, wipe your feet, put away your books, make your bed, bring down your dirty clothes, you can't have the car, why don't you ever stay home?, get off the telephone, don't chew with your mouth open and get your underwear off the floor'."

"Don't count on it," I smiled.

"Well, I hope he doesn't come," our daughter said. "You get flustered when someone knocks on the door collecting for charity and wants to be invited in. I can imagine what it would be like around here if you were expecting Robert Redford. You'd work us all to death," and she went upstairs to write in her diary that mom was having one of her spells.

"All I can say is, I trust good old Robert likes to spend money and smile. He'll certainly need a fat billfold and a sense of humor," and my husband kissed me lightly on the cheek and went to work to dream his own daydreams no doubt.

I have to admit it would take a little getting use to, living with a star. I don't know how a very ordinary, human-being person like me, could stand up to it..even if I tried real hard.

Why, Robert Redford doesn't have a gray hair in his head. I wonder what he'd expect me to do with mine? I'd probably have to sit up all night and pluck them out...one by one...as they came in. I never would get any sleep!

And I suppose he'd want a big breakfast. I doubt that I could palm orange juice and cold cereal off on him morning after morning. I bet he would look for hash browns and ham, served with a worshipful, bouncing, cheerful attitude and quite frankly, I don't know how I could rally around and be gay early in the morning after not sleeping all night.

And can you imagine borrowing Robert Redford's razor to shave your legs? I'd faint dead away the minute I picked it up and wouldn't be of any earthly use to anyone. Just the thought of having his toothbrush next to mine takes my breath away.

I'd have to sell all of our furniture, get rid of Augie-doggie and find friends who would take the children. You certainly couldn't expect a man like that to live in an atmosphere of grime and grouch.

Nor could you expect him to attend Junior High music programs or tolerate tuna fish. I'd probably have to quit smoking, polish my fingernails every day, speak softly, never cry real tears, give up my soap opera and learn to jog.

"He'd make you go on a diet," our son said. "Stars don't like chubby ladies. You couldn't eat dinner rolls or butter or mashed potatoes again for the rest of your life. You'd have to drink little cups of tea and eat watercress."

"There isn't a store in town that sells watercress," I told him. "Watercress is out!"

"And you couldn't scratch, sniff or storm around or story or stick out anywhere. And you could never, ever have mustard on your mouth."

"I don't get mustard on my mouth," I said. "Give me some credit. I don't need Robert Redord around to keep my face clean."

"You'd have to wear nicer nightgowns," our daughter pointed out. She was referring to my flannel nightie and fuzzy bedroom slippers. Ugly, but warm. "And you'd have to throw away those tennis shoes that look like shoe boxes. He'd never take you out in public like daddy does."

So far, I haven't a hair left on my head, I have no furniture, dog or children. I've thrown away every bad habit that keeps my life interesting, I'm starving to death, freezing and my feet are bare. My daydream is turning into a nightmare.

"And you'd have to like horses!"

Well, that did it. I hate horses. I'm not riding a horse for anyone...not even Robert Redford. I don't care if he gets down on his hands and knees. You can take your old movie star...I'll keep my plain, every day, comfortable, common, unstarlike, loveable husband any day.

Besides he's the best father I know.

"SOMETIMES A LITTLE BOREDOM WOULD BE A WELCOME CHANGE"

My husband never knows what his day will hold. "It would be boring," he said, "to be married to a woman who is predictable.". He tells me this but occasionally I see him glimpse dreamily at the ladies who stroll through shopping centers in high heels, fashionable skirts and carry small purses.

As far as I'm concerned those ladies aren't shopping they are just visiting.

In striking contrast I wear the loosest fitting clothes that taste will allow, sturdy flat heel shoes and tote a purse that hangs from my shoulder like a freight train. And I've never met a shopping mall that I didn't like...until recently.

It was a gorgeous thing. Magnificently constructed with marquee's announcing only the most exclusive shops. Native stone, splendid columns and the chandeliers I saw glittering through the spotless windows convinced me that it was a very special place. It definitely wasn't your ordinary sidewalk sale property.

I knew, of course, that I couldn't walk down its stately halls looking like a vacationing vagabond. A smock top and rumpled shorts were out. "I'll have to put on nice clothes, fix my hair and take a smaller purse," I told my husband. And most important of all I traded my comfortable shoes for heels that made me feel like a Queen. I could hardly walk but I was definitely taller and therefore, more regal.

I minced through store after store, in considerable pain, but putting on what I felt was a good show. My husband followed and was happy because I hurt so bad I couldn't beg for stuff. And I think he was taking some pleasure in being seen with a woman who didn't look as if she'd come in off the clothesline.

I can never resist a bookstore. And I spend a lot of time in them both personally and professionally. It's like walking into an old friend's house for coffee...I know I'm always welcome to stay as long as I like. We were thrilled to find a well-stocked bookstore in the heart of the fancy mall.

My husband shot off for the "Adult Eyes Only" section and I crippled my way toward the front of the store. Out of the corner of my eye I spied a large display rack, its brackets full of torrid, romantic paperbacks. Titles of love, hate and fury splashed out at me as I turned on my very high heels to find my husband so that I could confide in him that my feet were killing me and couldn't we go now.

Suddenly I was shackled to that wire rack. It was like one of the fictional lovers had reached from the book pages and grabbed my ankles. I couldn't move forward...I couldn't move backwards and I couldn't move sideways. The only way I could go was...down! And down I went. With no fanfare, no screams and with great astonishment I found myself flat on my back with 150 paperbacks on top of me.

"Help me, help me, help me," I cried.

My husband, his nose buried in a sex manual, was completely

oblivious to the fact his wife was being attacked by Harlequins; the salesclerk was busy somewhere else and although one or two passing customers paused in front of the bookstore and watched the chubby lady wrestling with 150 books and a wire rack they didn't want to get involved.

"Help me, help me, help me," I cried out again. This time a bit louder.

"Where are you?" my husband shouted. Thank God, he'd recognized my voice.

"Down here."

"Down where?"

"On the floor."

"What are you doing on the floor."

"Reading."

"Jeez."

"Help me, help me, help me. Please." I begged.

"I will when I find you," he promised.

"Look under the first big pile of books you find spilled on the floor and I'll be there," I snarled. He told me later my sarcasm hadn't been necessary....that he would've eventually found me. He said that he wasn't used to looking for his wife on a public floor and that he felt sorrier for the salesclerk than he did me when she discovered a fairly respectable looking woman in the act of destroying her store. He also said he was glad I wasn't hurt. I thought that was nice of him.

"At least you can't say you were bored," I told my husband later that evening.

"Sometimes," he sighed, "a little boredom would be a welcome change."

I don't think he really meant that...do you?

"TORCHING THE FRIENDLY SKIES"

My husband seems to think it's only fair I tell the world how I nearly single-handedly set an entire airplane on fire as it soared 39,000 feet in the clouds. I told him I didn't think it was anyone else's business.

"Never-the-less," he continued. "Perhaps if you'd confess it will prevent others from doing the same thing. You could save lives you know."

"Well, it really wasn't that difficult. Anyone could do it. It's not necessary to practice or anything."

"I still don't understand how it could've happened."

"It was easy. I simply got up that morning, looked in the mirror and said to my face. Good morning, my dear, this is the day you should set an airplane on fire."

"Be serious," he scolded. "You didn't do it on purpose. I remember how scared you were."

If he thinks I was scared...he should've taken a good look at the lady sitting next to me. Somewhere in the state of Montana dwells a perfectly sensible woman who now has skin the color of gray socks and hair that won't curl. Actually I don't even know why he brought up the subject. It's all over and done with and the fact my name is banned in the friendly skies and I can no longer board a plane without first signing a pledge that says I won't smoke if I'm more than two feet off the ground shouldn't be of any interest to anyone. Not even our children. Especially not our children.

It was an innocent accident. All I wanted was a cigarette with my coffee and the bag of treats the stewardess had tossed in my lap. She'd walked down the aisle, throwing those goody sacks like footballs, and after peeling mine off my forehead I pawed through it hoping to find something edible and non-fattening. Putting his away to eat later, my husband was napping and the lady sitting next to me nibbled delicately as she read a heavy romance. This left me, squashed in the middle, with snores on one side and passionate chewing on the other. I had nothing to do to amuse myself and was thinking perhaps I could work on the sweater, perched at my feet in a plastic bag, that I was knitting for Laura Elizabeth. I was quite bored, my ears popped like cannons and I was scared out of my wits.

So far I wasn't having any fun at all.

Scrunched like minced meat between my husband and the lady I knew exactly how a sandwich felt and as I dug into my purse for matches I could hardly bend my elbow, let along look sauve and sophisticated while lighting a cigarette. "And they say air travel is supposed to be a cultural and educational experience." I moaned. I wasn't even smart enough to light a match without it becoming a real challenge, I decided, as I lit two and watched them quickly go out as a whoosh of air hit them from the vent above my head. With deep concentration I shielded the next one by holding the matchbook in front of my face and puffing like the green dragon. I made one last attempt at lighting my cigarette.

This time it worked. In fact, it worked so well the entire book of matches burst into flames and I sat...stunned...with a fiery torch in my hands and no place to put it.

"Take it," I screeched tossing the whole hot thing in my husband's lap.

"ZZZzzzzzzzz," he answered.

Little crackles of flame crept quietly toward his belt buckle. My, wouldn't he be surprised when he woke up and found himself on fire. Quickly, before anything important could burn, I snatched the sizzling matches and turned to the lady beside me, who seemed to be in shock. "What'll I do?" I cried.

"Throw it on the floor," she cried back.

"If that plastic bag catches fire, Laura Elizabeth's sweater will be gone and so will we."

"I'm calling the stewardess."

"Don't you dare," I warned, "She'll throw me off the plane. I have seven children."

"That's your problem," and slumping over she began to hyperventilate. Resisting the urge to toss the whole mess in the long, blonde hair sitting in front of me, I threw it to the floor under the feet of the fainting lady and stomped with all my might until the flame was out.

"You've broken my toe," she gasped.

"A small price to pay," I snapped back.

"I'm telling."

"Please don't," I begged. "I'll show you pictures of my grandchildren." She sniffed a sniff and twitched slightly in her seat. This all occurred in about 30 seconds. Other passengers were unaware of this dramatic inferno and obviously the stewardess didn't suspect anything either because she approached the lady next to me, who now seemed on the edge of losing consciousness, to see if there way anything she could do to make her flight more pleasant. "Would you like another goody bag?"

"No," the lady said. "I'd like another seat." Apologizing, the stewardess told her we'd be landing soon and changing seats wasn't practical. "Just relax honey." she soothed, laying a kind hand on her shoulder. "Visit with her a little," she said, pointing to me. I was knitting like crazy and trying to look very dull. "Look, she's knitting a little pink sweater. I bet she's a grandma. And grandmas are always such gentle people."

"A lot you know," the lady said.

That was the end of any conversation until we had safely landed.

"I'll remember you until the day I die!" she screamed as I

prepared to leave the plane.

"Wasn't that a sweet thing for her to say," my husband smiled, as he steered me through the boarding tunnel. "It's always nice to make new friends when you're traveling."

A lot he knows.

"GOLF IS CRUEL AND UNSAFE"

I have discovered that few golf courses are built for pleasure. They are not loveable and they are not level. Most are a combination of the Colorado Rockies and Sherwood Forest with the Great Lakes scattered here and there. Toss in a flock of uncivilized, barbaric beasts and a homicidal golf ball and they can be downright dangerous.

My husband continues to insist that eventually he will teach me how to play a passable game of golf and that I will enjoy it or he will know the reason why. I keep telling him that my leg hurts, my back hurts, my arm hurts, my head hurts and there is no way I can possibly play golf in my poor physical condition.

"Why, I can hardly get out of bed in the morning, I'm in such poor shape," I whined.

"I noticed, I noticed," he said. "Nevertheless we have an investment in your golf future."

Good Lord, I thought to myself, you don't think that man is thinking about training me for the Dinah Shore Open. "What investment?" I asked apprehensively.

"Your clubs, the bag, the cart, the shoes and those little socks you wear," he totaled. "Those things cost money. We can't let them sit around and gather dust."

Recently we took a short trip to another state and as I eyed the quaint shops, the best restaurants and the fanciest night spots my husband ticked off the golf courses in the area.

"If we play 18 holes a day," he said, "we can try out every course around."

"Oh, goody," I shouted and prayed for rain. Oh, how I prayed. Every morning I looked out of the window of our motel room. I didn't brush my teeth, comb my hair or go the the bathroom. I ran to the window and begged to see wet. The sun beat down and the birds sang. The June weather was georgeous.

My husband danced about the room in ardent delight, clicking his cleats like castanets. He was in such a good mood he promised to rent an electric cart so that I wouldn't have to expend my energy walking but could conserve it for my game.

He was doing his best to make me enjoy golf and though I felt he had a long way to go I didn't say anything. After all, he has spent about 200 boring hours holding my hand in the labor room, the least I could do was spend a couple on the links holding my tongue.

My drive from the No. 1 tee went three yards. Everyone on the patio near the clubhouse laughed. I ignored them and swiveled into my seat in the golf cart and with a cosmopolitan air I waved my hand. "Take me to my ball, driver." I commanded.

"Everyone will think you're nuts if you ride three yards," my husband hissed.

"Who cares," I said stiffly and waved him on. If he wanted a professional, he was going to get a professional.

We wormed our way down the fairway. I was taking 10 shots to his every one. By the time we reached the fourth hole I had played a complete and par game of golf. And boy, was I pooped.

When I first saw the geese sunning themselves beside the water at the bottom of the hill I had no idea that they were killers. Frankly, I thought they were a lovely touch. A pretty addition to the scenery.

At that moment the good Mother Goose attacked our golf cart. She was having a giant temper tantrum right there on No. 6. She also had a wingspread of a 747 and the speed of a comet. Baring lethal goose teeth she honked her way straight for us. "She's going to kill us," I screamed.

My husband drove that golf cart like a hot rod. We careened across the course, running for our lives. "You left your ball back there," he yelled as we slid down the side of the hill. "That's $1.25 down the drain."

"You go get it," I yelled back, clinging to the side of the cart with all my might. I was bouncing very hard...and there are certain portions of my body that don't react well to bouncing. "Because I'm not going to."

As we neared the last hole, the temperature was starting to climb into the high 90s and so was my golf score. But I'd stuck it out and I was very proud. I was also nearly killed. I heard a shout and a torpedo-like noise in the air. For a minute I thought Mother Goose had returned.

A young man, screeching "Fore, Fore, Fore" was waving his hands frantically pointing at a white missile streaking straight for my head. Protecting my upper half I upended in the golf cart and exposed my bottom half. With a splat and a crack the golf ball hit my unmentionables. A perfect imprint of the ball throbbed on my backside. I wasn't mortally wounded but my spirit was broken.

"I'll make a deal with you," I told my husband as I stood in the golf cart on our return trip to the club house. "I will learn to play golf cheerfully if you will learn to disco."

He hasn't asked me to play since. Not once. I knew he wouldn't.

"GRANDMA VOLUNTEERS TO BABYSIT"

We're no different than any other grandparents. We volunteer to take care of our grandchildren sometime during the summer. Well, at least Grandma volunteers. Grandpa claims he had nothing to do with it and says that if Grandma peters out along about the fourth hour she has no one to blame but herself and don't count on him to bail her out. But of course, I do and of course, he does.

Frankly, I've never decided whether it's better to have them all come at the same time or divide them up in families. On one hand, the entire experience can be sloshed together in one horrendous, uproaring weekend or we choose to drag it out with two or three weeks in between to rest and regroup. Usually we settle on pinching in a little peace between visits.

The oldest grandchildren are girls...ages twelve and eight. The other family includes a five-year-old boy who thinks he's really Luke Duke in Jay clothing and a three-year-old girl with cherub cheeks and a mind like a steel trap. Laura Elizabeth isn't allowed so we don't count her. Not yet, anyway. But I think her day is coming. Last time I talked to her mother...she hinted.

Unfortunately, grandparents often become unprogrammed. Grandma is in the habit of leaving her sewing projects un-chaperoned on the coffee table and grandpa no longer adds suckers and gum to the list when he runs to the grocery store. And both are quite accustomed to having a solid night's sleep without interruption.

"What if they wake up and I don't?" I asked my husband when the brother-sister set checked into "Grandma's Motel" for the weekend. Visions of our home being dismantled in the dark of the night by an insomniac and industrious Luke Duke crossed my mind.

"Once they get to sleep," he said. "Their mother promised they wouldn't wake up." Wonderful! But no one told me how to get them to sleep in the first place. Round eyes stared at me from beneath the covers. "Aren't you sleepy?" I asked our little grand-daughter. She'd been as busy as bread dough all day, rising to occasion by jamming a year's adventures into only a few hours. "Grandma is sleepy," I yawned and stretching out on the bed beside them I proved my point by shutting my eyes and feigning sleep. Two thumbs and six fingers pried my eyelids open. "I see you Grandma," she shouted, her face two inches from mine. Indeed she did. partially blinding and deafening me in the process.

"We need a story," our grandson said.

"I've already told 64 stories," I groaned. Goldilocks had pig-ged out on so much porridge she must weigh at least 350 pounds; Sleeping Beauty had been kissed by the Prince so many times it was becoming obscene and Chicken Little was punchy from being bounced on the head. Our grandson said he thought they were pretty dumb stories anyway. "Tell us about monsters," he begged.

"I don't know any monsters."

"I do."

"Name one," Grandma was becoming a bit punchy herself about now.

"Grandpa!" His little sister nodded her head in absolute agree-ment. "Yah!", she said seriously. "Grandpa is a monster." Now, don't get them wrong. They loved their grandfather very much. Circumstances had clouded their attitude. I had definitely warn-ed my husband that he shouldn't paint our front porch ten minutes before they came, expecting them to read a "Wet Paint" sign. I told him pre-schoolers couldn't read and to them the sign might as well say "Slop and Smear."

It was when Grandpa discovered bits and pieces of tiny, gray footprints romping through the interior of his spanking new car upholstery that he became slightly monsterous and mostly faint and I have to admit that his roar sounded pretty authentic and I suppose to a tot, watching a grown man flail his arms and stomp his big boots, it could possibly constitute the picture of a monster in their mind. I gave him a pretty wide path myself for a while.

Perhaps a snack would help them sleep, I thought. They'd been eating steadily since 8 a.m. but one last bribe shouldn't hurt. "Grandma will fix you a nice lunch," I offered.

"Oh no!" our granddaughter cried...her rosy cheeks puffing in and out in pure horror, "It's too dangerous!" Admittedly, I'm not the world's greatest cook...but dangerous? Grandpa thought that was so funny he apologized for yelling and told them a hair raising tale about giants and dragons that feasted deliciously upon little children that didn't read signs and pay attention to directions from their kindly grandfather. They loved every gritty word of it and it wasn't long before they had snuggled down and in three minutes were fast asleep. We didn't hear a peep out of them all night.

The next morning while they were enjoying their breakfast of orange soda pop and black licorice I praised them for being so good and told them they could certainly come back again.

It wasn't until they'd left for home that I went into our guest room and found those funny little gray feet marching across my best bedspread.

And Boy! If you want to talk about monsters....you should've checked out grandma.

"GRANDMA AND GRANDPA ENTERTAIN"

Grandpa had just dug up his good tools from the cellar where he had hidden them during a visit from a pre-school pair of grandchildren; repainted the front porch to remove their tiny footprints from the previously freshly painted surface; retrieved Tippy the cat from the top of an oak tree; cleaned the Kool-aid from the windshield of his car and sighed "Isn't it nice to be old and alone."

"Not for long, sweetheart," I called out as another daughter drove into the driveway, depositing five suitcases, two sleeping bags, eight stuffed animals, Barbie dolls, roller skates, boxes and boxes of table games and her two daughters, ages twelve and eight.

"Good-bye," she cried out merrily and backing out to quickly return to her own quiet home and happy husband she called over her shoulder...."have fun!"

"I'm bored, grandma," the twelve-year-old said.

"Me too," whined her sister.

"Goodness, you just got here," I reminded them. "We'll find something fun to do."

"What?" they cried in unison.

"We'll pit cherries," I suggested.

"Ugh!"

"Pick cucumbers?"

"We don't want to."

"Weed Grandma's flowers?" The eight-year-old began to cry.

"Mama said we were on vacation," her pretty sister explained. "Mama said we wouldn't even have to make our bed at your house. Mama said she didn't when she was a little girl."

"And did mama tell you what happened when she didn't make her bed?" I was sure she hadn't. "Why don't you go see what grandpa is doing."

"Oh, we can't do that" they trembled. "Grandpa's in the bathroom, laying on his back with his head behind the stool. He's saying bad words, there's icky stuff on the floor and he waved a big wrench at us. We don't want to go see grandpa right now." I didn't blame them a bit. So we sat cross-legged in a circle and played jacks and they laughed because grandma couldn't get past the twozies. Nor could I get my legs uncrossed.

"We'll play a stand-up game, grandma," they promised, huffing and puffing, as they pulled me to my feet. "We'll play hopscotch. Can you play hopscotch?"

Of course, I could play hopscotch. Wasn't I the champion of southern Illinois in my day.

The fact that this day was a long time ago probably had something to do with my back going out as I stood on one foot, forehead pressed to the ground trying to snatch up a stupid rock. "I'm bored, girls," I sighed. They were having a hilarious time watching grandma making a fool of herself on the front sidewalk.

"Why is your forehead so red?" my husband asked as he walked out to join us.

"Can we go to the bathroom, now, grandpa?" the little one asked nervously, searching his hand to see if he was carrying a big wrench.

"Yes, you can, honey," he said sweetly. "But promise grandpa you won't try and flush your sister's Monopoly money away again. Remember, it's only a game...and someone has to be a loser." And then he said if we'd all get cleaned up he'd take us out to eat and then for a game of miniature golf. I persuaded the eight-year old she should wash her face, kindly reminded the twelve year-old that she was far too young to wear her aunt's false eyelashes and told grandpa that no, we absolutely could not stop with young chilren for twofers in a cool lounge.

"We'll choose a family place," I said firmly and sadly, he passed by those restaurants featuring prime rib and a piano bar and stopped at one sporting a large cow with an ice cream cone clutched in her right hoof.

"This won't be good for my ulcers," my husband complained as he scanned a menu full of calories and pure cane sugar. But as I pointed out, they too, offered twofers.

"On lemonade," he growled. The two little girls asked why grandpa was so cross and if this meant the golf game was off. I assured them that grandpa would be fine as soon as he found out how cheap it was to eat in a restaurant that catered to children, cane sugar and lemonade and sure enough, by the time we left my husband was smiling again and had quit holding his stomach.

We discovered that our twelve-year-old granddaughter was a whiz-bang with a golf club and beat us 17 out of 18 holes; the eight-year-old had a tendency to fudge on her strokes and that mosquitoes that hang around miniature golf courses are bigger than the golf balls. By the end of the evening grandma and grandpa had been humiliated, cheated and chewed and grandpa was sloshing from so much lemonade he was accused of making funny noises in the car and the two girls rode home with their heads out of the window.

Thank goodness, they told their mother they had a lovely and exciting time and she promised they could both come back real soon. I can hardly wait.

But grandpa's not so sure.

"A MOTHER'S SPECIAL HANG-UPS"

When our children were small, their summer vacation often stretched before me like a limp string. It seemed dull with no interesting knots.

Invariably, I developed a series of personal hangups.

"Hang up your jeans," I cried. "Hang up those bathing suits! Hang up the towels! Hang up that baseball cap!"

"Someday, mother," our oldest daughter complained, "you're going to slip and tell me to 'hang up' my little brother. And I am."

At least I'd know where he was. A major problem was keeping track of everyone. I put the baby in the playpen. I knew she wasn't running from neighbor to neighbor begging for cookies. I wasn't sure about the others.

Nothing ever happened the way I'd planned. My good intentions would've filled a suitcase. I made lists, wrote notes and looked in the encyclopedia for pertinent information to liven up our lunch and dinnertime conversations. I was determined our children would accomplish memorable things to take back to their classrooms in September.

"Listen up, everyone," I cried. "The boll weevil is an insect of the beetle family."

"Who cares?" our son said as he grabbed his little sister's hot dog and held it high above his head, teasing her into a major fit.

"The boll weevil has a long snout..."

"Like hers..." a daughter interrupted to point directly across the table at the 15-year-old. A soft slap, slap, slap followed.

"Stop it right this minute," I shouted.

"I'm taking my coffee outside," my husband said with a weary catch in his voice.

"The boll weevil lays hundreds of eggs," I doggedly went on.

"Is this a sex story, mommy?" our first grader asked. Her interest peaked at this point. "My teacher said we're too little to know about sex."

"Listen to your teacher. She's right," I said.

"I heard you tell daddy my teacher hadn't been right about anything in 40 years."

"I was wrong."

"I heard you tell daddy you hadn't been wrong about anything......"

I shushed her by explaining in vivid description terms how the boll weevil mama often fed on her young.

"Mother, that's awful," the 15-year-old ceased slapping and moved a protective arm around the tiny girl.

"I'm sure there are case histories, as well, where parent-bugs eat big kids," I closed that day's lesson with determination to find a more acceptable activity for the next day. I choose arts and crafts. I would keep hands busy and make time fly usefully.

"Today," I announced brightly, "we will spend the afternoon making mash."

"We're going to make whiskey? Wow!" The twelve-year-old's eyes sparkled. "We can set up a stand. I bet we'll sell more of that than we did that sour lemonade you made us peddle last week."

Ignoring him, I explained we were going to create beautiful objects d'art by learning to create with papier mâché. "That is why we will spend the afternoon making mash."

Actually, I spent the afternoon making mash. Our children disappeared one-by-one. Only the baby stayed and spent an exciting hour watching through the bars of her playpen as her mommy cooked shredded paper. I boiled the strips of paper for the required time and then whipped it until it was soft and pulpy, just as the directions said. Placing it in a strainer, I squeezed gently until the pulp was a moist lump. Putting it into a bowl, I stirred in white glue and mixed with all my might.

"Uhhhm, that looks great, honey," my husband said bending over to kiss me on the back of the neck. "Something good for dinner? It sure looks yummy. Is it a new recipe?"

I resisted the urge to dress it up with parsley and serve it in a nice dish. Instead I placed it on the counter and overnight it turned into gray cement. I threw the whole mess, bowl and all, into the trash. So much for creative summer fun.

"We'll be practical from now on." I promised. "The boys can chop wood from the forest and the girls can make soap."

My husband pointed out that the nearest forest was probably 10 miles away and by the time we bought the necessary ingredients for soap-making, we could buy a years supply of readymade bars. "Why don't you let the children play house and climb trees?"

"And waste a whole summer? It wouldn't be right." I said.

"What did YOU do during the summer when you were little?" he asked.

Sheepishly, I admitted I played house and climbed trees.

"You turned out okay," he said smiling. "Prolific...but okay."

That's when I quit making lists, writing notes and looking things up in the encyclopedia. I tossed my good intentions out with the mash and taught the baby how to patty-cake.

"At least she's learning something useful," I thought.

As for the others, they played house, climbed trees and forgot to hang up their clothes. I continued to yell and scream and my husband often drank his coffee outside under the cherry tree.

It was one of our best summers.

I hated to see it end.

'LITTLE LEAGUE MOTHERHOOD"

Medical books list thousands of diseases-incurable and otherwise. They have, however, failed to mention one...one, that unless cured in its earliest stages and by drastic prescription can be close to fatal. It is called "baseball."

I am not speaking of the kind of baseball I was raised on as a child: The Professional vs. the Professional. I am speaking of the kind we were exposed to as parents...when our sons reached the magic age of participation..the Awkward vs. the Awkward.

It is called Little League. There is no known cure. But who wants one? Not me.

You see, I love baseball. My dad had taken me to ballgames for years. While most little girls were raised on lollipops and doll babies I grew up with popcorn and the St. Louis Cardinals. I learned to keep a box score before I learned to play hopscotch. Instead of puttering about the kitchen baking brownies I was taught to appreciate a double play. My hero was Dizzy Dean and my vocabulary included adjectives directed at the umpire. Not very ladylike but an awful lot of fun.

But I was not prepared for Little League. I don't think any mother is.

Nor was I prepared for the fact my husband was harboring secret desires to manage a baseball team. I don't think any wife is-any smart wife anyway. Actually, smart wives and mothers avoid Little League games like poison. They stay home and placidly mend and wash uniforms, make home-made root beer and pretend ignorance of schedules and practices and team standings. Unfortunately I have never been considered smart. I never missed a game. I suffered terribly.

My husband's previous attitude about professional baseball

had been neutral. If the teams were tied, the bases loaded, a muscular pitch hitter up to bat and the World Series was involved, he might stir up enough interest to ask the score. He did not understand why I sat in front of the TV chewing my fingernails or why I threw the dishtowel at the radio when a home-run hit was caught or why I drug him to see the St. Louis Browns (now dead) while we were on our honeymoon. He just did not understand.

Neither of us suspected that he had, floating around in his bloodstream, the germs of baseball. It was just that they lay dormant until our sons reached the age of Little League. Then they burst forth from him like the plague.

"Mom, mom!" our sons cried the day they came home from their first tryouts. "Dad's going to be a manager!"

Shades of Casey Stengel. I thought he had been elected President of the United States. They couldn't have been happier-or prouder if he had. I eventually was to discover that to his baseball team and their parents he was more important than the President of the United States. And made as many mistakes too.

My husband had no alibi. He admitted being caught up in the enthusiasm of the crack of the bat. Besides, he said, no one else would do it. I certainly believed that!

"Actually," he went on to explain, "it shouldn't take up much of our time. A game here and there..practice now and then."

That was a lie. You all know that. Throughout the summer our garden grew at random, unattended and uncultivated; windows filmed over with build-up grime; we didn't take a vacation; kissing was replaced by batting averages and we ate so many weinies-on-the-run that I become nauseated at the sight of a mustard jar to this day. Our summer was baseball and the Little League.

And I have to admit...it was fun. Sometimes!

I learned many, many things that first year. I learned not to yell at the umpire under any circumstances. The first time I screamed..."Blind-good grief-you are BLIND" at the gentleman behind the plate he turned around and gave me a long hard look. It was the local optometrist up the block who prided himself on his 20-20 vision. And because he was not earning a fabulous salary as a volunteer daddy umpire he was more than happy to jam his mask, chest protector and shin guards into the hands of any loudmouth mother that thought she could do a better job. I never razzed an umpire again. Well, hardly ever.

I also learned not to say anything about the child who had just swung for the third time at a ball rolling on the ground. There was a 50-50 chance his mother was sitting directly behind me-waiting for my son to miss an easy pop fly because he was sitting down in left field tying his shoe or looking at butterflies.

There is little doubt that one of the highlights of my past summers as a Little League Mother was grappling for splinters after the game ended. Those wooden bleachers were murder. How I wished for cold, slick steel. My husband told me if I would just sit still, keep my mouth shut and not get so worked up I wouldn't get all stuck up with splinters. I told him that this was not easy to do with two player-sons and a manager-husband on the field for God, our neighbors and the umpires to judge and assess.

From experience I learned a Little League combination mother-manager's wife has a special function to perform. She could perform this function much better if she had no tongue and was physically invisible. She has to be Supportive! And Loyal! And Crazy! And she can't look over her shoulder when she hears the words..."dumb managers!"...or "What does he think he is doing now?"...or Why is my son sitting on the bench?"

Instead, if she is smart, she will hope nobody recognizes her and cheer for the other side.

It was not hard for me to cheer for the other side. Not hard at all. I had known some of those little boys since they were born-changed their diapers too-and just because they had "Tiger" stamped on their chests and were on the opposite team did not keep me from an appreciative cheer when they blasted what turned out to be a grand slam homer in the infield. My sons and their father did not think this was at all necessary. They did not go so far as wish a "boo" out of me...but I'm sure they thought the least I could do is keep my mouth shut. But I never did.

Our family played every game about three times. Once on the diamond, once on the way home in the car and a very thorough deep discussion outside under the Chinese elm after dark. Every boy was analyzed and a solution sought on why this one dropped that easy fly or why that one couldn't throw any better than their five-year-old sister or why some of the boys batted like girls.

I resented this and took it personally because I could remember a girl in my fifth grade class named Loretta who could hit harder than any of the boys in our class or the next. Most of them would have given their knickers to have been able to slam a ball like she did. She was our big bat. Secretly I felt my husband's team might have been better off to have a few Lorettas and not so many Irvings. But at that time the government had not discovered equal rights, and no one paid any attention to girls...let alone grown-up mothers...when baseball was discussed. It was truly a man's world-except when they wanted their uniforms washed. I am glad to say this feeling has changed. Maybe the Lorettas of the world will finally get their chance.

For awhile I had trouble understanding that nine-year-old boys did not take the game as seriously as their parents. I had to learn not to become overly nervous because the shortstop's glove was too big for his hand and kept slipping off at crucial moments or that the pitcher had difficulty getting the ball to the plate or that the first baseman's "stretch" measured about four inches, give or take a little. I was no different than any other parent. I had high hopes of nurturing an instant George Brett the minute our son put on a baseball cap. I had to lower my standards. I sort of knew they were too high when the first game they played lasted three hours, the score was 20-0 and the first inning was still in progress.

I once knew a lady that was banned from watching Little League games when her son played. It was not me. And it was not the league officials, the fans or her son that banned her. It was her husband. I just know it was her husband.

For years this lady never talked in public. Never said a word beyond "hello." And sometimes she just nodded her head and didn't speak at all. Then she attended her first Little League game. She found a whole new world. She also found her vocal chords. She began to chant, to yell, to scream, to swear, to offer an opinion.

Her husband was in shock. He was losing control. His wife was developing a personality. He soon stopped that. He wouldn't let her come anymore. Made her stay home and needle-point. I missed her.

And I have to admit...I miss Little League. Our son's are grown now. There are no more spikes in their shoes; no precious gloves to be oiled with loving care; no triumphant slides into homeplate; no more teary-strike-outs; no more trips to the root beer stand; no more admiring glances from their sisters and their friends as they put on that dashing Major League uniform for the first time; no more sloppy sharing at the water jug with comrades; no more kisses from mom when they lose; no more handshakes from dad when they win...no more victories...no more defeats.

Or maybe there are. Maybe some memories never end. Maybe they learned about "life" in the Little League.

I know I did.

"RINGING THE FAMILY BELL"

Recently, I received some comments from a sweet young mama who explained she was bringing up her children in a neighborhood of grandmas and grandpas. "Their families are all grown and gone," she wrote. "And most had the opportunity of raising their kids in the country where screaming couldn't be heard and hot wheels were unheard of. I'm an ex-cheerleader and my voice carries for miles. Sometimes, I think I shock them."

Hey, I know exactly what she means. Try having seven children (all under twelve) in an area where planned parenthood was a popular hobby.

Like hers, our neighbors were tolerant, sympathetic, understanding but shockable. I often saw imprints of rose bushes upon their behinds proclaiming the obvious...they'd been sitting among the thorns...again...protecting prizewinning American Beauty roses from our three year old son's tricycle. As my correspondent pointed out, hot wheels hadn't been invented. I think I'm glad about that.

Now my husband and I are a part of the older generation and I smile behind my hand when the little four year old from down the block stomps onto the porch and asks if my "kid" can come out and play. The "kid" is looking sixty in the eye and has trouble bending over to tie his shoes but he goodnaturedly shares a glass of lemonade with her as they sit and chat about L-I-F-E.

There are moments when I see the dark curls and the not-so-dark graying head bent together discussing tea parties, football and the adventures of Scooby-doo when I'd love to do it all over again. We have such good memories.

Then when I can sit down at 9 p.m. without having my legs ache from chasing toddlers all day, and know that I don't have to get up to fetch anyone a glass of water, scrub out a gummy bathtub, throw in a load of wash, or read "Goldilocks" for the 9,000th time...I know, for sure, that I'm glad they are only good memories and not raw reality.

I, too, was a mama excheerleader and my vocal chords were stupendous. I could shake the leaves off trees when I stood on our front steps and screamed our children home. My husband, whose mother was a lady, couldn't understand why I had to yell so loud.

"Tell them what time to come home," he said "and then expect them to obey."

Four couldn't tell time, none had workable watches and one was a dog.

He realized the futility of his suggestion and fearing that I'd lose my voice and he would have to represent the family on the telephone, he bought me a Captain's Bell for Mother's Day. Hanging it on the front of the house, he insisted it would solve my problem.

He was absolutely right. When I rang the bell, Lueth kids came streaming from every direction. Even Augie reacted to the bell and appeared, tongue lolly-gagging and sides heaving from his efforts to reach the yard before any human critters.

Promptness brought a pat on the head to each and all; laggers were likely to get the hands-over-the-hips-where-have-you-been routine.

The bell called them for meals, bedtime and to find out who'd carried off their dad's best screwdriver. Meandering about the neighborhood was allowed as long as no one went beyond the sound of the bell. It was a real lung saver and no one under voting age was allowed to touch it without permission.

Only the Very Good Child was given the privilege of ringing the bell for mom. It was sort of a prize, handed out for outstanding behavior. One son, who leaned toward pranks, edged with a slight tinge of devilment seldom had the opportunity. Even after earning his Bachelor's Degree he continued to claim his prime ambition in life was to ring Mom's bell.

His sisters and brother howled with laughter.

By the time our oldest daughter was exploring the dating game, she could tell time and had a nice watch that worked. She promised to observe a reasonable curfew, if I promised to keep my hands off the bell. It was a fine arrangement and seemed to be working well.

Until one night. I was startled to hear the midnight silence broken by the loud peeling of the bell. Who was ringing it? Certainly, not me. The other children were in bed. Augie was snoring with his nose under my chair. Was it ghosts?

I crept out the front door, picking up my trusty broom along the way, fearful that I might see something supernatural tugging at the leather strap. I was prepared to beat to death the person or persons ringing my bell.

Thank goodness, I looked before I smashed. It was my husband. We'd failed to let him on the pact and when he'd observed two heads very close together in the front seat of the car parked in the driveway, he'd resisted the urge to hit our daughter's date on top of the nose and hit the bell instead.

The reaction of the occupants in the automobile was much the same as it might have been had someone struck a match over the gas tank. They exploded from the front seat. I waved them back with my broom and Mr. Date made a hasty retreat out of the drive and our daughter ran to her room to cry for 14 years.

Eventually, she stopped crying long enough to marry this same young man and to this day, if someone accidentally brushes against the bell and it tinkles, his face turns dead white and he shows signs of bolting.

Oh, yes, I kept the bell. I don't use it often but once in awhile, if the "kid" gets out of my sight...it comes in handy.

You see, the bell is not only good for wandering children...it works on husbands as well.

"A TRUE-LIFE FAIRY TALE"

Once upon a time there was a Little Princess with golden curls, cherry red lips and one tiny molecule of mischief buried deep within her baby-soft body. She was a Country Princess. Acres and acres of cornfields and waving grain surrounded her castle. It was her empire to rule and she took her position seriously, rising early to her tasks and retiring late. The Queen Mommy often wondered if the Little Princess bothered to sleep at all.

King Daddy sometimes shook his manly head in astonishment that such a small person could have such energy. "Why does she play 'ring around the rosie' with such vengence?" he asked the Queen Mommy. "I can endure eighteen holes of golf without taking a second breath but running around in circles for 375 consecutive times poops me out. Does she not know any nice sit-down games?"

"Pray thee, don't ask me," the Queen Mommy said.

The Little Princess smiled her secret smile and once again, taking King Daddy by the hand led him around and around and around until his eyes crossed.

"Something must be done," he puffed. "I can't keep this up. We will have to find her another playmate."

Queen Mommy nodded wisely and said "We have."

Six months later another Little Princess entered the Farm Castle. Her name was Lacey. But alas, she was much too young for the Older Little Princess to play with.

Not that she didn't try mind you. Oh, but she did. The baby Princess was astounded to find her rattles turned into tom-toms on her tummy; her clean wash cloth was used as a bonnet upon her head and when the Baby Princess slept, which she frequently did in self defense, it wasn't unusual for her to have both eyes pried open with demands that she wake up and play.

"This isn't the solution," King Daddy sighed. "What will we do now?"

Queen Mommy put her thinking cap on her pretty hair and sat down in her rocking chair. She thought and thought and thought. "I know," she jumped up and clapped her hands. "You must find the Little Princess a pet."

"Good idea," and King Daddy called a neighbor with a mama cat and quickly a playmate kitty was carried home in a sack. It was named "Friend" and mewed gently when placed in the Little Princess's arms. It seemed the perfect solution. The King Daddy and Queen Mommy relaxed and enjoyed their peace and quiet.

A few hundred circles later, Friend Kitty no longer mewed but loudly protested with sharp claws and screeches. It seemed to say "I will not allow anyone, not even a Little Princess, to shanghi me, pull my paws apart and run me around until I'm dizzy. I'm going to split," And he did.

It was a sad day in the Country Castle. The Little Princess cried large, salty tears and King Daddy resumed his position as the number one playmate and again, Queen Mommy put on her thinking cap.

"I have an idea," she said a few hours later. "I think it will work."

"It had better work," King Daddy cried out. He was turning green from going around and around and around. He did not look well at all.

"All fairy tales have a wise Fairy Godmother. I will go right now to the telephone and call her. Surely, she will help me out." The Queen Mommy dialed long distance and spoke to the Fairy Godmother. She listened and nodded. Hanging up the telephone she took the King Daddy's hand. "According to F.G. we must make a wish," she said.

"What should we wish for?" the King Daddy asked.

"How about a microwave?" Queen Mommy grinned.

"Don't be silly!" The King Daddy's face grew bright pink.

"I know what we'll do. We'll close our eyes and wish for the Royal Grandparents to visit over the Fourth of July holiday. They love the Little Princess. They will be glad to come and play with her."

The King Daddy and the Queen Mommy sat down, held hands, crossed their fingers and their feet and wished and wished and wished. Together they said "Oh, please make our wish come true, Fairy Godmother." You could hear the Fairy Godmother laughing her head off.

Now the Royal Grandparents lived in a tumble-down palace in a far-away land. They were no longer young but had retained some enthusiasm for life. The Royal Grandma could not see without her spectacles and the Royal Grandpa could not hear unless someone stood on his toes and spoke directly into his face. They were prone to short (but interesting) naps throughout the day. It was their only social life.

They lived in seclusion with no Little Princess's and Prince's of their own and only shared bed and board with a blue-blooded cat named Tippy and a semi-precious dog called Augie. Each morning they woke up and smiled at each other because they knew they no longer had to buy fourteen dozen toothbrushes a month and eat weinies.

But one day in July, The Royal Grandmother answered the telephone. It was the wise Fairy Godmother.

"Hi there, kiddo," the Fairy Godmother said and the Royal Grandma remembering the times she had called on the Fairy Godmother herself, listened carefully.

And if you want to know if the Queen Mommy and King Daddy got their secret wish...you'll have to read the next chapter!

"THE LITTLE PRINCESS TRIUMPHS!"

In their tumbled down palace in the faraway land the Royal Grandma and Royal Grandpa were playing a grand game of Scrabble. The Royal Grandma was losing.

Gleefully the Royal Grandpa collected his tiles and spelled the word "Phlegmy" The Royal Grandma had no idea if he was spelling it correctly. She was quite relieved when the telephone rang and interrupted the game.

It was the Fairy Godmother asking for a favor.

"The Little Country Princess needs you," the Fairy Godmother explained. "She's very lonesome. The King Daddy and Queen Mommy have played 'ring around the rosie' so much they are beginning to twirl in their sleep. They sent out a regal S.O.S. They need your help."

"You can count on us, Fairy Godmother," and the Royal Grandma knew she'd been saved from being humiliated. Adjusting the frayed velvet around her throat, she assumed her best your-humble-majesty voice and approached the throne where the Royal Grandpa was happily adding up his score.

"Sir," she said, bowing slightly at what was once her waist, "We have been given a command for an audience with the Little Princess at her Country Castle. We must leave at once."

The Royal Grandpa grumbled something about the Royal Grandma always quitting when HE was winning but dutifully put away the game because he, too loved the Little Princess very much and could not bear to see her sad.

"While you gas up the chariot," the Royal Grandma suggested. "I will run to the market place for gifts."

Obediently, the Royal Grandpa did as he was bidden. Taking the chariot, he filled it with unleaded and put air in the tires. It only took a minute. He was back on the front porch of the tumbled down palace having a tankard of iced tea when the Royal Grandma came huffing and puffing up the sidewalk.

"I've found the perfect present for the Little Princess," she gasped, "but I couldn't carry it. You will have to go forth and pick it up. It is a molded plastic swimming pool. It has blue bubbles and green mermaids dancing inside. The Little Princess will love it."

"It will not fit inside the chariot," the Royal Grandpa said.

"Oh, but it must," the Royal Grandma put her hands on her hips. She was getting quite red in the face. The Royal Grandma liked to get her own way...especially when it came to buying gifts for the Little Princess. "You can squeeze it in. You can do anything." She turned to the Royal Grandpa and patted him nicely on the Royal Tummy.

This gave him incentive and he said "So be it."

Placing the Royal Grandma in the front seat of the chariot, he put the large, plastic unbendable swimming pool in her lap. She could not see out of the front window; she could not see out of the side window. All she could see was blue bubbles and green mermaids. It was very boring.

The Royal Grandpa complained that the other driver's on the King's Interstate looked at him like he was a crazy man because he seemed to be carrying on a conversation with a large plastic swimming pool.

The Royal Grandma waxed something poetic like "Tough!"

The Royal Grandparents didn't even stop for lunch. Even when the Royal Grandma complained that her left leg was cramping badly. The Royal Grandpa wickedly set his teeth and said "If you think I'm pulling into a resaurant along this King's Interstate and having anyone see that an actual person is silly enough to ride beneath a plastic swimming pool, you are out of your Royal Gourd." And that was that. The Royal Grandma had learned over the years to keep her mouth shut on certain occasions.

My, how the Little Princess loved her new swimming pool. She hugged the Royal Grandpa's neck and kissed the Royal Grandma's cheek. This made everything worthwhile. Having people think you are a fool and sweating, starving and cramping beneath blue bubbles and green mermaids seemed inconsequental. The Royal Grandparents looked at one another in a smug manner as the Little Princess played 'ring around the rosie' and splashed all at the same time.

"If you understood Little Princesses like we do," they said to the Queen Mommy and King Daddy, "you'd have no more riddles."

"Just wait," the two of them chorused. "Do not count your chickens until they are hatched."

"Fiddle-faddle," the Royal Grandma and Grandpa said in unison.

Time passed and the Little Princess grew tired of the plastic pool. It was left to gather fallen leaves and swimming spiders. She concentrated all of her efforts on the Royal Grandparents. She did not allow time to hang heavy on their hands.

When the alloted hour for their visit to end arrived, they were allowed to return to the tumbled down palace in the faraway land. The Royal Grandma sighed three times with pure exhaustion as she waved goodbye from the speeding chariot. The Royal Grandpa said they would definitely hang up on the $!?&/- Fairy Godmother if she ever called again.

When they finally reached the tumbled down palace, the Royal Grandpa found he'd wrenched a hip from too many turns at 'ring around the rosie' and the Royal Grandma had ten layers of silver nail polish on her toes.

Back in the Country castle, the Little Princess, worn out and tired, snuggled down in her bed, fell asleep and dreamt that everyone in her entire kingdom lived happily ever after.

I have no doubt that they will.

"I BEAT YOU HOME AGAIN, MOM!"

By the middle of August everyone at our house began counting down. Thoughts turned toward new shoes and pencil boxes. Hurrah! Soon school would start. For the most part our children were always ready and eager. As for me...I was more than ready. I was practically hysterical. I'd survived June and July. All I had to do was get through August.

An old hand at preparing children for kindergarten, I patiently explained for the 200th time to our sixth child that mommy was not planning to throw her to a gang of witches but sending her into a shiny and bright experience. I promised she would have a peppy and pretty teacher who would let her color and sing. "You'll learn nice games and how to print your name," I predicted. She said she already knew how to print her name.

"But this will be fun. Trust me. You'll like it."

She continued to think I was trying to get rid of her and that morning answered the telephone by saying. "Hello! My mommy is mean to me today."

I hastily explained to the gentleman caller that I was only preparing her for kindergarten...not man-handling her. "No problem, lady," he said. "She made my day." I was glad someone was having a good one.

Throughout the entire month of August I pumped her full of merry stories and cheerful anecdotes until both our heads were spinning. She was beginning to doubt my authenticity as a truthful mother. Her older brother didn't help. "Don't believe her, kid," he warned. "Once you walk in that door, they never let up. You'll be going to school for the best part of your life." He was in Junior High and faced a math teacher with the reputation of a snapping turtle. Personally, I thought she was terrific and exactly what he deserved.

Wearing the traditional new dress and scared look, she took my hand the first day of school and I walked with her to the playground. Pausing, she drew my head down to whisper, "I don't think I'll go today. I'll come home with you and we'll color in my coloring book there."

Gently, I told her she had to grow up and go to kindergarten. I left her looking very much alone and stopped off for coffee and consolation at a neighbors. When I arrived home twenty minutes later, I found her sitting on the front step.

"I beat you home, mommy," she smiled proudly.

When we moved her closet from home to her dorm room at col-
ege she was eighteen years old. I assured her it would be a
marvelous adventure. "It will open up a whole new world for
you," I guaranteed. She said she liked her old world just fine,
thank you.

Quietly, I told her she had to grow up and get on with her
education.

That afternoon she introduced us to her new roommate by saying "This is my father and this woman claims to be my
mother...but I've never been so sure about that."

Her helpful brother had confidentially confided that once we
left her on the campus it would be "out of sight...out of mind."
This wasn't true, of course, and his only basis for such an
assumption was our refusal to send him hundreds of dollars in an
envelope every three or four days. "Don't pay any attention to
him," I said. "You're only 80 miles away." I tried hard not to see
the tears gathering as we said good-bye. We stopped for dinner
and when we arrived home found her sitting on the front porch, in
the dark, waiting for us.

Explaining that a friend with a car had decided to spend one
more night in front of the home fires, she tagged along. "I beat
you home again, mom," she laughed. Indeed she had.

A few weeks ago we accompanied this same daughter to a
midwestern state to further her education. The college was
located in a very large city and the metropolitan flavor seemed
overwhelming. We went for miles without seeing one cornfield
and when we drove up in front of the tall building where she was
to live, I gulped once and said "It's a good thing you are a mature
adult now. You'll probably love this once you get used to it."

She gulped twice and looked at me as if it had all been MY idea
instead of hers. "I'm not sure I'm going to like this," she groaned.

"We'll stick around until you get used to it," my husband promised and for three days we toured, shopped, walked the streets
and clung to her like parental ivy. By the end of the third day we
were all exhausted from so much togetherness but I was hesitant
to leave because I could remember her brother's prediction and
parting shots as he hugged her good-bye. "If you can make it
through the first six weeks without being attacked," he said
seriously, "your chances will be pretty good. You'll be street wise
by then."

I was prepared to stay for the full six weeks but my husband
said we couldn't afford it. He reminded me that she was now
definitely old enough to take care of herself.

We promised to write and call often and my last glimpse was one of a forlorn figure, standing on the sidewalk, looking as if she'd just lost her two best friends.

"I wonder if she'll beat us home this time," I sighed. My husband happily said that he wouldn't be surprised. It took our combined efforts not to turn around and tell her we would save her the trouble of trying.

Turning into our driveway, I wasn't at all shocked to see a shadowy form on the front porch.

"She didn't," my husband laughed.

"She might!" I anticipated, jumping out of the car and running to the house ready to give her a warm greeting.

But it wasn't her. It was a sister, who'd patiently been watching and waiting. "I thought sure she'd be here before now. I miss her so." We all did.

However, it's certainly a good feeling to know we finally have a grown-up daughter...even if it does hurt a little.

"SLIPPING INTO SEPTEMBER"

Recently I read a syrupy article about September. It spoke of the frenzy and fuss of the coming fall months following the long, leisurely summer. I don't know about anyone else but I didn't have a leisurely summer. I agree that it was long but if I remember correctly most of it was spent trying to get teenagers out of bed in the morning and into bed at night.

The article suggested that we take time to relax and smell the smoke of autumn..."Try on your favorite wool skirt," it said,..."join an exercise class; plant colorful tulips, crocus and narcissus bulbs; finish that sweater you started to knit on July 4th; sit down and order tickets for a concert; plan a day for you and your teenage daughter to shop for fall clothes-have a fancy lunch together; adopt the stray cat the summer people abandoned; cuddle up with your husband and sip Irish coffee; put up the storm windows before it freezes and remember to send this season's most colorful leaf to a friend as a gift."

I didn't think those suggestions sounded so bad so I immediately went upstairs and tried on my favorite wool skirt. If you didn't count the moth holes, that skirt looked pretty darned good after spending the summer crumpled up at the bottom of our closet. The fact that I couldn't get it up past my knees told me I should probably sail right by wool skirts into exercise class...before I smelled smoke or anything else...but my recent bout with Aerobic's were still fresh in my mind...and my bones.

"Perhaps I'll just skip wool skirts and exercising," I told my husband, "and try planting tulips, crocus and narcissus."

"What happened to the $300 worth you planted last year?" he asked.

"Something must have eaten them," I suggested. "Probably something deep in the ground with sharp teeth and a craving for tulips, crocus and narcissus. And one did come up, don't you remember?"

"Oh, you mean that poor little stalk leaning up against the porch. It didn't bloom."

"I didn't promise blooms," and I turned quickly to the sweater I'd started knitting on the 4th of July. It had four rows and 18 dropped stiches.

"Honey," my husband said. "You'll never get that done in time for Christmas."

"I'd like to," I smiled sweetly. "It's for you." His face turned the color of egg yolk. "Are you going to be sick?" I asked, peering into his eyes. He shook his head and sat with his face in his hands.

"It says here I should order concert tickets," And scanning the area newspapers I told him we had three choices...two rock concerts, a night of Blue Grass and-or Gospel.

"Forget the concert tickets," he groaned. "I'll struggle along with football two or three times a week and call myself cultured." I frowned at his obviously weak character and turned to the list. The next possibility for pepping up September concerned a teenage daughter, shopping and a fancy lunch.

"Well, you can certainly scratch that one," I said with straight-lipped determination." I did that last year and my back hurt for a week from stress. She didn't get any fall clothes and I didn't get any lunch."

My husband said he couldn't understand why the two of us couldn't get along in public like normal people and I said if he wanted her to go shopping so bad HE could take her and he said that he didn't think it was really necessary for anyone to buy clothes at our house for at least five years and I said and he said.........

I didn't think it was the proper time for bringing up the adoption of a stray cat!

It was a bit difficult for me to find a leftover cat on our block anyway because we didn't have any summer people. Everyone lived in our neighborhood all-year-round and only left for two weeks to go on vacation. But I told my husband I was obligated to look for one.

"Bring another cat into this house and it won't be the only one classified 'abandoned', believe me when I say that," and he stood firmly in the doorway, one hand on the latch and the other on my suitcase. Augie stood solidly paw-to-paw behind him.

I wondered if an abandoned mother would have as much trouble finding a home as a cat. Surely not, I thought...I could always go live with our older children. My husband laughed out loud when I told him that.

I was near the end of my list. So far, I didn't think the prospects of a cool September looked so hot.

"Do you want some Irish coffee and cuddle?" I yawned a few hours later.

"I'm too stiff," my husband moaned. Bless his heart, he'd spent nearly all day putting up storm windows. "You'll have to decide between cold air and cuddling. At my age I can't do both." And you'll just have to guess which one I chose. But I can tell you this...a little autumn chill never hurt anyone.

I was finally at the end of the list and as I tried stuffing a crunched oak leaf into an envelope for two friends celebrating a 25th wedding anniversary, our youngest daughter peered over my shoulder. "You aren't going to send that mess, are you mom?" she asked. "That's dumb."

It may be dumb...but it's certainly cheap. I wonder if I'll get a thank you note?

"A HOUSE CAN BE A LONELY PLACE"

It was only day before yesterday that I tied yellow ribbons in our youngest daughter's hair, packed a little schoolbag with pencils, tablets, hankie and a dime in case she needed to call home.

She was too small to reach the telephone, had never dialed in her life, but I felt better knowing she had some money if she needed it. I walked her to kindergarten and she was sad when she said good-bye.

Two weeks ago she went to college. There were no yellow ribbons because I haven't been allowed to touch her hair in years. The schoolbag was replaced with four suitcases, eight packing cartons, several appliances and three blank checks...all signed by her father.

I tried slipping a dime in her pocket and she laughed, telling me I probably needed it worse than she did. We walked with her to her dorm room and she could hardly wait for us to leave.

My husband and I are adjusting to being alone but our house is in culture shock. "Why am I sitting here, tidy and clutter free?" the living room cried out yesterday. "Please look under my couch to see if there are any dirty dishes."

Mrs. Table Lamp sputterd and assembled her watts. "I'm worn out with all this clicking on and off," she flickered. "Why can't I just burn for 48 hours straight like the Good Old Days?"

The television, shifting it's cable, agreed. "I hate this," he crackled.

"All I'm getting now are soap operas, westerns and Johnny Carson. At least, I used to have a little variety. A few cartoons, some violence and once in awhile, a bit of sex. It kept life interesting. These two old people are pretty boring."

"You can say that again," Stereo woofed. "Have you caught the music they've been playing on me lately?" If I hear Andy Williams sing 'Moon River' one more time I'm going to blow my tubes. I'd give ten tape decks for just one Yah-yah-yah and a screech"

In the kitchen, the refrigerator grumbled and piled up more ice cubes. "God, I'm freezing to death in here," the butter shivered. "When the kid was home I could count on a breath of warm air every 15 minutes when she opened the door hung on it and yelled 'Why isn't there ever anything to eat?' Now they're on a diet and all I've got to talk to is cottage cheese. I really miss those Dilly Bars. They were sweeties."

"At least she isn't scrubbing your enamel off," a hot voice whined. Standing over in the corner, Miss Stove spit out her pilot light. "I don't think I've cooked anything but green beans and liver for days. If I could only heat up one hamburger I'd be happy."

"Hey, you two get a load of the dog." The kitchen table stirred once and scraped his legs. "He's been under here moping with his head between his paws until I could collapse right on his ears." A waxy tear slowly rolled across his shiny table top. "And I have to wear these fussy place mats with napkin rings yet. I saw the fat lady throw every paper plate and plastic glass in the house away and heard her say something about 'Now, we can live with a little class!' That'll be the day," and the table kicked until there were only two chairs left standing by his side.

The telephone was fighting for it's life as a million busy spiders built homes in it's silent dial; the shower croaked with rust and the bathroom stool yelled out "If something doesn't happen pretty soon, I'm going to forget how to flush!" In an upstairs bedroom it was deathly quiet as two teddy bears clung together for comfort.

"Did you hear something?" the Dryer asked the Washing Machine. They were standing, polished like white rocks, in a utility room free of sock box, smelly sweatsuits and Shrinky Dink T-shirts. They looked lost and more rested than they'd been in years.

"I think it's Old Brown Car," the washer said. "He's crying."

"Why should he cry?" Miss Dryer fluffed. "A month ago he was complaining because he couldn't stay still long enough to have his tires changed. Personally I'm enjoying not having to roll my drum every five minutes. This has been the biggest lull in my life and I'm going to take advantage of it. I hope I never have to dry blue jeans again as long as I live." The Washer looked sheepish and admitted that she missed the jeans. "All I wash now are boxer shorts and pantyhose with a load of bathtowels now and then. It's not much fun being a washing machine if you can't fade anything." The two of then snuggled up against the wall and fell asleep.

Inside the garage, Old Brown Car, drooped his license plate. "If I don't get out of here soon," he roared, "I'm going to drop a gear."

"Ha," Green Bicycle rattled his chain. "I don't know why you're so upset. I've been sitting here all by myself since she turned 16. Look at my handle bars. They've rusted clear through to the bone. Now it's your turn. See how you like it!" Old Brown car said he was not going to put up with it another day and planned to sneak out that very night and run around the square and blow his horn. "And end up in jail," Green Bicycle sneered.

I told my husband everything seemed so strange around here now that she's gone. "Even the house is acting funny," I said.

"The poor thing is lonely," he answered.

And so are we.

"THE FAMILY THAT RAKES TOGETHER — STAYS TOGETHER"

During the past month my friends and neighbors have attended bazaars, teas, style shows, football games and some have even gone to Las Vegas and Boston. I've spent the entire month of October raking about 18 million leaves. Next year I hope our trees go stark naked all summer.

I do love trees, and I treat them right, by golly. I feed the little birds and squirrels and I encourage owls to hoot upon their boughs. You'd think they'd have a tiny bit of respect for me. The least they could do is spit in the neighbor's yard.

But it doesn't work that way. Every leaf in town has taken it upon themselves to find their way into our yard. The first one fell three blocks away from our house. I saw it on one of my daily walks. It was laying there, damp and crumpled. By the time I returned home it was crunched down by our front porch near the sidewalk.

"Where did you come from?" I asked, picking it up by a limp stem and tossing it into the garbage disposal. I probably shouldn't have done that. I probably should have handled it with more reverence and taken it into the house, mounted it on construction paper and taped it on the living room wall for everyone to see and admire. Instead I killed it and relatives came from miles around to take their revenge.

From that day forward our yard became a dusty family reunion site for approximately 860 species. I could hardly open the front door.

"Where did this birch leaf come from?" I wondered as I shuffled my way into the house. "The nearest birch tree is clear across town."

"If you think that's bad," my husband said, scratching his back and pulling the foliage from three oak trees out of the neck of his sweater. "Here's a Bonzi sprig."

"Good Lord," I screamed, "That means they're coming from overseas. We'll have to do something fast or we'll be buried in hostile tree leaves. We might not be found until spring."

"The children would miss us," my husband soothed.

And speaking of children, I'm sure you are wondering what happened to that good, oldfashioned picture of a happy family gathering leaves to run and romp in while cold cider and doughnuts waited deliciously on the sidelines. I would bet that visions of this delightful sight crossed your mind. They crossed mine too. I called our oldest daughter and her family and invited them to spend the day with us.

"We'd love to," she said happily. "The girls will really like that. They've been wanting to visit grandma and grandpa."

"Wear old clothing," I said slyly.

"Why?"

"I'll give you a hint. We're having doughnuts and cold cider."

"I still don't understand," She sounded puzzled.

"Don't ask! Just mind your mother." And because she's always been an obedient and respectful child they came, dressed in sweatshirts and old jeans.

"Hello", I said as they came in the door. "Did you have a nice trip? Have you had lunch? Have a doughnut and here's a rake...let's get to work." The four of them looked stunned as I handed tools all around. Perhaps our son-in-law was the most surprised. For some odd reason he'd planned to spend his Sunday afternoon watching football and drinking a beer or two. Instead, he found himself hauling 14,000 black trash bags to the ally with a stale doughnut between his teeth.

"I don't like to do this, grandma," our seven-year-old granddaughter sneezed.

"Will we get paid?" the ten-year-old wondered. Grandpa assured her that the "Leaf Fairy" might be able to come up with something. Our son-in-law didn't look quite so sad.

"Dad, you don't have to pay them," our daughter said as she crawled beneath a prickley evergreen shrub to ferret out bunches of dead elm leaves. "It's good for them to learn to help the elderly without compensation." Now my husband looked sad.

Being called elderly didn't bother me in the least. If I had to fall in that category in order to rid myself of the mess in the yard, so be it. I'm not above cashing in on my age when it comes to help-outside-the-house. Or inside-the house for that matter.

Eventually we finished. The yard looked great. True, my husband didn't look so hot, our son-in-law was very cross, our daughter was scratched up and exhausted and the two little girls threw up because they'd eaten too many doughnuts and drank too much cider but I was pleased and very contented. However, I had to promise that I would sit on our front porch with a shotgun and shoot down the first leaf that fell on our lawn.

But I don't think that's asking too much...do you? All I can say is—don't come by our house and flutter like a leaf—it could be very dangerous.

"COME JOIN THE CLUB"

In the past thirty years I've taken classes that dealt with crocheting, knitting, aerobic dancing and cooking. I even sat in on five sessions supposedly concerned with teaching me how to make a sport coat for my husband. That was eight years ago. Need I tell you that $75 worth of material, thread, interlining and a stuffed "ham" for pressing purposes still grins from the depths of my closet...untouched, unsewed and unworn by my husband. It's a subject we don't talk about around the house. Well, HE talks about it but I don't. Someday there will be a demand for maroon and gray plaid texturized polyester and the kid will be ready.

Therefore with all the courses I've taken I really think I've become an expert and could start my own classes. And I will be the teacher.

"What do you know enough about to teach, mom?" our son asked as he watched me busily go about the business of preparing brochures, planning my advertising campaign and working on promotional material. "What could you possibly tell about that would interest anyone?"

Each member of our family watched in suspense as I tacked a large cardboard poster on the wall, displaying an obviously relaxed and happy mother as the center of attraction. She had her shoes off, wore no lipstick, her left hand held a small glass of wine, her right hand clutched a candy bar and her hair needed combing. And there wasn't a child in sight!

"Classes held every day," the poster proclaimed. "No tuition. No registration. No certification. No diploma. Hours are from 4:30 p.m. until 6 p.m. You don't have to do a darn thing to qualify. No books, No lectures, No demonstrations. Bring your own bottle and cheese. Ice and crackers furnished. Babysitters are NOT available and if anyone mentions what they are having for dinner they are immediately expelled." I stepped back proudly and admired my handiwork. I was tired but happy.

"I don't think anyone will come," my daughter said. "It looks boring."

I doubted that. I recalled the millions of mother hours that have rolled by in the dirt during the "witching hours" between 4:30 and 6 p.m. It's the most confusing time of the day. Too early for evening activities and too late to start a daytime project. That's exactly when Augie-doggie decideds to throw up, my prettiest plant dies, the aluminum siding salesman knocks on the door and I discover there's no flour to thicken the gravy.

If I'm going to have a sick headache I have it between those hours. If I'm going to break out in hives I'm going to do it then. The windows become noticably dirty, the cupboards crumby, the faucets drip and spiders hold a square dance on the ceiling. Babies are at their crankiest; preschoolers lose their shoes; elementary children get bloody noses; Junior Highers smoke their first cigars and this is the time when the Senior High student chooses to tell you that he is flunking geometry.

It is the longest ninety minutes in history of time.

"You might concentrate on dinner preparations," my husband signed.

"How much time does it take to ruin a roast?" I asked. "I can't cook for an hour and a half."

"Take a walk," he suggested.

"And have the neighbors wonder why I'm not home cooking. Not on your life."

"Write a letter."

"No one answers my letters."

"Ride the expensive bicycle that you could not live without."

I groaned.

"You can watch cartoons with me," our youngest daughter invited.

"I've seen them all...twice!"

There was nothing left for me to do but drum up something that not only I could enjoy but I could have congenial company around me while I enjoyed it. Chewing my pencil I knew that because our organizational lives today are programmed for dues and good deeds I wanted a group structure that did absolutely nothing.

There will be no election of officers, no talk of politics, no weigh-ins (heaven forbid) and by-laws will be non-existent. There will be no pledge of allegiance to the flag, no cheerful songs or dedications. No cookie committees, calling committees or membership committees. No doilies, tallies or rallies. And absolutely no name-tags. You won't have to tell anyone who you are and if you want...you could even make up a name. I don't care. No one will call roll and if you're absent that's your tough luck. You won't have to say why you aren't here and you won't have to provide a handwritten excuse.

There will not be a dress code either. Wear your best finery if you want to show it off but if you feel more comfortable in ratty jeans and a sloppy sweatshirt please feel free to come in those. There will be no group pictures taken so who cares how you look. It is an open invitation to anyone that wants to attend.

However, if you drop by and I'm not home...come in anyway! The door will be unlocked. And if you get bored, remember, the mop is in the utility room, the vacuum in the closet and there's a couple of cleaning rags hanging on the line.

So don't just sit there...do something constructive!

"WHY I NEVER MISSED A PARENT/TEACHER CONFERENCE"

Now that school is in full swing and mama can safely put away bathing suits, chewed thongs, too tight summer shorts and break out sweaters and wool, I have a few observations left over from my own days of hustling kiddies out the door early in the morning.

It's a bit like childbirth and your first blind date. You never forget! And after it's over, you don't want to repeat it. At least, not in this century.

Parents and teachers have one goal in mind. The child's welfare. I've never doubted this for a minute. But I always wanted to invite the teacher into our home so he or she could see the real me instead of the imaginary one they conjured up in the teacher's lounge.

"Did you see the Lueth kid this morning?" the teacher observed as she reached for another tasty cookie, sent by the Lueth kid's mother in a paper sack as a birthday treat. "His fingernails were dirty and he had two different colored socks. Do you think she's playing with a full deck?"

(The truth was..our son had been bathed, groomed and scrubbed with loving maternal care the night before. He had a worm farm in his bedroom and chose that particular morning to cultivate his little spread. As any good farmer-person knows it's hard to mess around in the dirt and come out squeaky clean. As for the socks...well, if they'd taken a quick look, his brother had on an identical pair.)

"The sixth-grader keeps telling me the dog eats her homework. That's the oldest excuse in the world."

(The truth...the dog REALLY did eat homework. As well as potted plants, straw baskets, toothbrushes, cardboard boxes and ice cubes.)

"The youngest one forgot her Weekly Reader money again. She said her daddy screamed and said he was going to the poor house if the school didn't stop asking for money."

(He didn't scream. He simply stated a fact. Perhaps, to a 6-year-old it sounded like screaming. I don't know, however my husband is a kind man who for years, sported raw fingertips from hauling nickles and dimes from his pockets each morning before we sent the children to school.)

"Speaking of the father. Do you remember last year when the boy brought the dribble glass for Show n' Tell and claimed it was his dad's Most Precious Possession. Until that day, I'd considered him the most stable one in the family."

(The dribble glass had been left at our house after a neighborhood block party and just happened to belong to the fellow down the street who was employed in the Administrative Offices of the school system.)

"The last time we had a PTA meeting not one member of their family showed up. Our room lost the banner. SHE wrote a note and said they were all sick. I didn't believe it."

(Believe it. At that point of my life a PTA notice was like an invitation to a Royal Ball. If you didn't count doctor appointments it was the highlight of my social life. We were sick. Possibly due to the fact the chicken pox was stalking school corridors and our second-grader had been thrown up on by the kid in front of him, the one in back and two on each side.)

"It doesn't surprise me that they are ill. Did you see the one on the playground without a warm coat! She said her mother lost it! Can you imagine...losing a child's coat?"

(Not lost...misplaced. And she was offered a perfectly good substitute but refused to catch the bus if I made her wear the in-house spare. Could I help it if this jacket had raccoon fur on the lapels and no buttons? To me...warm is warm. To a child, frost bite is preferable to being teased by classmates. And it only happened once. Well, maybe twice.)

"They told me at the Junior High school she washed the oldest boy's football uniform and the pants came back as pink as a pretty rose. He had to play four games in those awful rosy pants and the opposing team took turns gang-tackling him."

(I apologized to the principal, I apologized to the coach, I apologized to our son for those dumb pink pants. I even offered to foot the bill for new ones. I learned a valuable lesson. Never wash a purple blouse with football pants and don't trust a football coach that laughs out loud in your face. Our son also learned a lesson. He gave up football and turned to the Fine Arts.)

"And remember when she took a car full of students on a field trip, got lost and didn't bring them back until after we'd called the police?"

(How was I to know when they told me we were going to a chicken house they meant a Poultry and Feed store and not Kentucky Fried. That little trip cost me $14 in meals and the embarrassment of being frisked in public by the local men in blue.)

"Do you think she'll show up for Parent-Teacher Conferences?"

(You bet your life! I wouldn't have missed them for the world. It was my only chance to tell the other side of the story.)

And if I were you...I wouldn't miss them either.

"I LOVE FOOTBALL"

Some people follow rainbows...I follow football. I love it. This doesn't mean I always understand it. At least, not altogether. But then I don't always understand my husband and children either and I love them.

My pulse beats faster, my glands swell up and my toes throb to the cadence of the marching band as it takes to the field prior to the game. I throw my whole heart and soul into the toss of the coin. I'm the first to stand for the Star Spangled Banner and the last to sit down after the kick-off. I shout plaudits and praises to players and coaches alike...on both sides. I'm excited and enthusiastic. I'm a fan!

"But you don't watch the game," my husband said.

"Of course I watch the game," I replied, slightly insulted.

"Then why do you always ask me what happened?"

I told him that people attend football games for different reasons. I told him we don't all go and sit hunched over and grumble and sulk and not talk.

"I talk," he said.

"Sure", I admitted. "You talk. You talk to the referees. But they don't talk back. They can't hear what you are saying."

"Thank God," he said.

I don't think it's really necessary to attend a football game and completely forget the social graces. I think it's perfectly OK to say hello to a friend and ask questions about their children, their homes and their bridge game. Even if I have to turn around and yell two rows up...I don't think that's so bad. It's outside and everyone expects shouting at a football game.

A friend attends because she has no choice. "I go because my husband keeps telling me that if I'm exposed enough I will catch the disease. I've been attending football games for 30 years and I still can't tell who has the ball."

"I will help you." I told her. "I will explain the game."

My husband snorted. Her husband snorted. I didn't pay any attention to them.

"It's sort of like cooking," I told her. "Everything is all mixed up but each ingredient is important. Take the two units for instance. The offense and the defense. These are entirely different."

"I know that," she said, "but what do they do?"

"It's like this," I explained. "Pretend the offense is the salt. They make the game taste better because they score. The defense is the pepper. They spice it up because they punch out the other teams."

"Oh," she said. "I see. You make it sound so simple. But I still don't know who has the ball."

"It's really not that important," I told her. My husband choked on his popcorn. "All you need to know is which end of the field your team is supposed to go. If your whole group only moves a teeny bit duck your head and mutter...if they all go roaring down the field like crazy then stand up and wave your arms like a maniac and whoop! This means they are probably going to make a touchdown."

"How will I know when they do?" she wondered.

"The man in the striped shirt will hold up both arms in the air like he is praying and the cheerleaders will do a routine."

"You mean I don't even need to know who the quarterback is?"

"Heavens no," I told her. "I can never find him. But I know his mother."

"Isn't that nice," she smiled. My husband groaned.

"It's impossible to see anything that's going on and understand when they are all huddled up like that in the middle of the field. That's why I only watch when they spread out a little."

"What do we do in the meantime when we aren't watching?" she wondered.

"Well, we can talk about people," I suggested.

"I'd like that," she said happily. "Football really is fun. I certainly can't see why my husband didn't explain it like this 30 years ago. Think of all I've missed."

"You're going to warp that woman," my husband whispered

and her husband tried to sit between us. We ignored them and
continued to enjoy the game. We discussed many things. We
talked about our children, detergents, the lady-of-the-town with
the subtle reputation, the price of groceries and gas, our
neighbors, our golf game, new fall styles and the weather. It was
an interesting game. In fact, we were so involved she gave her
husband's seat away at half-time when he left to get coffee. He
told her he was not happy about that.

He told her he had to stand down on the sideline and missed
most of the second half action. My husband went with him
because he said he couldn't stand one more minute of my in-depth
football.

When the game ended we asked our husbands who won the
game and we vowed to meet again.

"I love football," she said. "I can't wait until next week."

It isn't so hard to be a fan after all...now is it!

"GYM BAGS REALLY DO STINK"

I ran into a mother younger than I am (which in itself is not
unusual as most mothers I find are ALL younger than I am) and
she had a request.

It concerns gym bags.

"Why haven't you written about gym bags lately?" she asked.
She looked pale.

"Because I do not write dirty stories," I answered.

"But I need help!" she cried. She has three sons. All of pre-
bacteria or full-bacteria age. "When you wrote about them
before, I just whipped through that column. My sons were still
playing cowboy. They weren't carrying gym bags."

I nodded sympathetically. I knew just how she felt. Even
though our son's gym bags have been replaced by massive laundry bags that only come home from college once a month, the
smell's the same...and the memory is there. It will never leave my
brain buds. They have been permanently damaged. The odor will
line my nostrils forever. Never again will I benefit from the sweet
smell of a rose or the delicious aroma of freshly baked bread. On
the edge of everything I sniff is the hot, moist smell of the
swamplands-or worse!

"Just the other day," the poor young mother said, bringing out a dainty handerchief and automatically placing it over her quivering nose, "our oldest boy accidentally left his gym bag in the car, unzipped just enough to let off pressure."

"Actually you should be grateful for small favors," I said, patting her arm. "It could have exploded and blown up if he hadn't left an escape valve."

"But he left it there all weekend and the windows were rolled up. You can't imagine what happened when I first opened the door on Monday morning..."Her voice trailed off into a whimper. She threw her hand to her forehead and sunk into a chair. The poor woman was distraught. She was REALLY distraught. "Our insurance agent said he wouldn't pay a cent. In fact, he threw up in the driveway. He may sue."

I didn't ask her if the car started. I didn't want to know. A woman can take only so much before she breaks.

The gamey smell of a gym bag has to be the major thing that bothers mothers. But there is more. Oh yes, there is more. You knew there would be.

I, for one, have a very difficult time identifying and properly recognizing the very odd things that are in gym bags. You see. I grew up in a household of sisters and a shy father. I did not know one intimate thing about boys. I only knew what I saw in the Montgomery Ward catalogue. And in my day they were very careful about what they put on their glossy pages. Only manikins wore underwear!

But, boy, I got my education. I certainly did-when our son's started to carry gym bags. In fact, it was up to me to go shopping with them to buy all the stuff they needed. I didn't even know what to ask for. Neither did they. And what they did buy, they put on backward. That was certainly funny. Not to them-not to me-but their father thought it was hysterical.

"I don't think you should laugh," I told my husband. "It could hurt their psyche or something."

"Just be glad they had the initial 'try-on' at home instead of the locker room," he giggled.

"Oh I don't know," I pointed out. "Coaching has to have some rewards."

Over the years I have learned the names of almost everything they have in their gym bags. I have also developed my own method of dealing with this masculine laundry. Quite frankly, I open the washer, stand in the middle of the room and stiffarm the whole mess into the machine. I do not sort. I just throw.

And I let it soak. I let it soak for at least three or four hours. At the end of this period the inside of the washing machine looks like black-gumbo and smells worse. I used carpet shampoo and wax remover mixed in with a strong, low-suds detergent, sit back and pray. What has not disappeared altogether comes out passably clean...and certainly smells a lot better. I can vouch for that.

Quite often, however, I shrink things. And I have yet to figure out how to shrink the boys back into the article of clothing that is now a few sizes too small. But I'm working on it. And the first problem I am going to solve is shoes. Football shoes. Expensive football shoes. Naturally, I do not wash them. They just shrink all by themselves. The more they cost the quicker they shrink.

Personally, I have never been able to understand why boy babies weren't born with cleats on their feet in the first place. I feel this is a practical idea. Maybe some mother younger than I could work on it. I have no intentions of having any more boy babies...with or without cleats.

It was a terrible sight watching our son hobble around the house two games before the season ended in football shoes three sizes too small. Those shoes were a virtual vice and made his tackles a thing of pain to watch.

But I usually let him suffer, for in some small way this sort of made up for the gym bag.

"THE PITTER-PATTER IS GONE"

Since our children are growing up I hardly see them. Oh, I know they are around...I can tell by the toothpaste smatters on the bathroom mirror...but I mean in the flesh, touching hands, exchanging conversation.."See them."

"I haven't seen the children lately, have you?" I asked my husband.

"I think I saw one of them thumbing through my billfold a couple of days ago," he answered. "But I'm not sure...it was dark in the room. It could have been you."

Honestly, he has the strangest notions. He knows I wouldn't do that...at least, not so he could ever catch me.

Just as I grew used to living in a house with jelly on the woodwork, diapers in the washing machine and tic-tac-toe on the windows and accepting it graciously, suddenly and dramatically things changed. The whole atmosphere of our house has become morose, mute and much too big. I am not sure I like it this way. Not like I thought I would.

"It is so quiet here," I complained to my husband. "And it is boring. Nothing is going on. The house is like a tomb."

"Don't knock it." He stretched, grinned and stroked the television set. Monday night football romped across the screen uninterrupted. No one was fighting for their life but the losing team's quarterback; no one was kicking and screaming but the cheerleaders; no one was throwing anything but a football. No one was home.

I know they have been there. I can tell. I can tell because the stereo is still panting and my Andy Williams records are warped. I can tell because there are no potato chips or pop left in the house and the sugar-coated cereal boxes stand in the cupboard with the tops open and the popcorn popper lid has been put away greasy.

I can tell they still drop in at home on occasion because the shower continues to foam at the mouth with shampoo and nearly every electrical outlet serves as an umbilical cord for a blow-dryer and the interiors of the upstairs closets are gradually being eaten away with unwashed tube stocks.

Here is a dirty flannel shirt with the pocket torn, a tennis shoe with no survivors, a lint-covered Certs, four pair of wrong-side-out jeans, a punched out cafeteria ticket and a yellow cloud of spray cologne hangs from the ceiling like smelly smog. No, they have not left entirely...it is simply now that they are growing up I never meet them face-to-face.

"It is like we have an invisible family," I sobbed. "I just see their remains...I never see them."

"Remember when you used to scream...I can't wait until they all grow up!" my husband gently reminded. "Remember when you were pottytraining you used to pray for puberty? Remember how you grumbled because you were the only lady in the neighborhood preparing banquet portions at every meal? Remember?"

I remember. And I still continue to fix meals for nine people. But now only three show up! Me, my husband and Augie-Doggie. And the three of us are rapidly gaining weight because of it. Of course, it doesn't show up so much on Augie...his hair just fluffs out more-but my husband and I are having real trouble.

I cannot bear to put four tablespoonsful of peas in a pot. As far as I'm concerned if you can't throw in a couple of cans, it isn't worth turning the stove on.

Faithfully I fry 12 pork chops and mash a pound and a half of potatoes. I am expecting 18 feet under the table. I salt and pepper in innocent abandonment. And then I get telephone calls and handwritten notes that say..."Will not be home to eat. I will be home early."

One has gone to play football; one has gone to play volleyball; one has gone to play at a friend's house; one has gone to play tennis; one has gone to play at a part-time job; one has gone to play at baby-sitting and one has gone to play at heaven-only knows-what. There will be four feet and four paws under our table and I have prepared enough food for 15 people. I do not take this well...not well at all.

The stove trembles as I stomp around the kitchen, waving a large fork and a whirring hand mixer. My apron is crumpled and red spots have appeared on my cheeks. The kitchen curtains are limp from steam coming from both nostrils and tongue. And then my husband comes home. He is expecting to sit down with his little family for a peaceful meal and meets a mad woman at the door.

"It happened again," I yell, "No one will be here for supper but you and me."

"Augie is here," my husband points out, his indigestion on the rise and he hasn't even eaten. Augie is sitting patiently by the pork chops, his eyes watering from pure greed.

But he is definitely not going to get those pork chops. Not tonight. I might slip him a pea or two but he is not getting that expensive meat. I'm saving it for tomorrow night...or the next...if necessary. We will eat it then.

But I suppose the children won't be home to eat then, either. And I don't know how long I can safely serve those pork chops.

So, if you don't have anything better to do in a couple of days, along about suppertime, drop on over. We're having leftover-leftovers. We always have room for another set of feet under our table.

"I REALLY DO ENVY TEACHERS"

I really do envy teachers!

Now, in my mind's eye, I can see 20 of our children's past educators whispering..."Who does she think she's kidding?" fourteen nodding in unison and agreeing that the Lueth lady has finally flipped; twelve putting fingers down their throats going "gag, gag, gag," and one or two smiling secretly because they know exactly what I mean.

Even the veteran of 30 years must feel the excitement of stepping into a freshly scrubbed classroom on the first day of school to face a brand new bunch of youngsters dressed in their September best. If, by some stroke of fate, each student shows a high degree of individual independence, responsibility and good manners, the teacher knows this school year will be a breeze. I can only guess-but this must be the same sort of sensation and relief received when an impacted widsdom tooth is removed.

But surely there are times when they hit a snag. That's when they dust off their badge of courage, step to the front of the room and say in a commanding voice..."Attention, please! I am your teacher!" Underneath they could be asking "Why?"

I think I know!

A chance to eat in the school cafeteria every day? I don't think so. The opportunity to watch the new crop of seventeen and eighteen year olds sporting "Hurrah! I'm a Senior!" tee shirts? Probably not. Helping 26 kindergartners find their mittens? No! Anticipating hostile Parent-Teacher conferences? I wouldn't bank on it. Taking tickets at the football games? Not the social event of the season.

Why then? In all likelihood, it's because they hope to become millionaires before they retire. (Again I can hear "Is she kidding?" along with 75 percent jamming fingers down their throats while the other 25 percent lay comatose on the floor of the teacher's lounge.)

Not millionaires in the dollar sense, of course, but millionaires in memories, merit, many-sided skills and marvelous accomplishments. I've never met a teacher I didn't like. Well, maybe one.

I can only imagine the diplomacy an elementary teacher must have to tactfully suggest to a ten-year-old that it is mandatory that he change his underwear at least once during the semester term; compassion that must be felt for the unfortunate second grader who doesn't own a Cabbage Patch Kid; the craftiness of persuading a little one that his original portrait of mother must be preserved in the teacher's desk and not displayed on the bulletin board for everyone to view mama's bald head, prominent teeth and dress made up of nothing more than red spangles; the technique of explaining to this disappointed mother why Little Johnny's picture isn't up there with all the rest; the ingenious hiding of tears when day-after-day the wizened eight-year-old boy refuses to smile because his home life is a living hell and there's not much anyone can do about it. In that case, I DON'T envy the teacher.

There's no doubt a Junior High Instructor must, above all, have a great sense of humor and many-sided personality. They must be able to look like an authority figure and behave like a clown; able to freak out when they hear the same Knock Knock jokes a hundred times a week and not yawn in the teller's face when he catches them with "DuWayne the bathtub...I'm drowning." A merciful educator will also resist the urge to fill up a nearby bathtub and hold the jokester's head under.

Junior High teachers must also have the capacity to overhear some stories and not blush. It must be terrible not to be allowed to wash the thirteen-year-old mouth out with strong soap.

A gifted teacher won't laugh out loud when an eighth grader experiments with make-up and comes to class wearing every product Avon has produced in the past 24 years...all at the same time...and in some cases..all in the same place; nor will they snicker at the student who reeks of cigar smoke and has to lay his head down on his desk because he is deathly sick at his stomach. A practiced teacher knows this is only part of the growing-up game and accepts this along with the shy punches of cordial greeting from a student when they meet on public streets.

Elevated to higher learning a Senior High teacher often has to stand in front of his mirror and recite... "I do have a degree from a recognized university. I am smart. I am the teacher!" Possibly, this is due to facing a group of almost-adults who show varied signs of being more intelligent than the trained and experienced expert. An uncanny change has taken place. Often the students are taller, have better figures and can outrun the faculty in the hallway.

Perhaps the teacher has been attemping to grow a decent mustache for months, and failing, only to try and explain to a muscle-bound fellow with a full beard why Boy George probably doesn't equal Shakespeare in original verse.

Senior High teachers have the unique opportunity of watching tomorrow's leaders unfold like rose petals right in front of their eyes and have the good common sense and instinctive sensitivity not to hurry home and tell a spouse that the world is in real trouble. Instead they trust and have faith in their teachings. Sometimes, prayer doesn't hurt either.

Yes, I envy teachers. I wouldn't be surprised if many others felt the same way I do. Which brings me to my last observation and my last question...Have YOU hugged a teacher today?

"NAPTIME IS VERY IMPORTANT"

I remember my mother telling me that naptime for children was as important to their childhood as vitamins. "They must get their proper rest," she said as she placed our first born in my arms. "It will make them strong both emotionally and physically. And it certainly won't do you any harm either," she added with a twinkle in her eye.

This seemed logical to me so for the next 20-some-odd years when one o'clock came our children took a nap whether they wanted one or not.

"But mother, I'm sixteen years old," our oldest daughter complained when I pointed to her bedroom and said it was time for her nap.

"No matter," I said. "When you are in this house...you nap!"

"But I just got up."

This was true...she had just gotten out of bed but I'd been pounding the floor since 6 a.m. and I was weary. Therefore, it seemed only justifiable to me that our children were tired too. I operated on that theory during their growing up years. In fact, I operated on it until they married and had their own home. It was as automatic to me as fixing hot soup for lunch.

In the early afternoon all seven were banished to their bedrooms and Augie-doggie was unceremoniously tossed into his doghouse.

"Sleep!" I commanded. Some did and some didn't

What I didn't know at the time was the fact our children (and often the dog) were outsmarting me. This happens to mothers once in awhile. It was during naptime that our children plotted the strategy that made me so gray at a very early age..............

"It's your turn to chip a tooth," our son must have told his brother. "I did it last."

"But I cracked my elbow Tuesday," he whined. "Let her chip a tooth for a change." And he pointed across the wall to a younger sister.

"I'm not going to the dentist," she shouted through the thin partition. "Maybe we can get Augie to lose a tooth."

"Dad won't pay for a dog's tooth," someone pointed out.

"We could all get the flu."

"Then we'd have to throw up and then mom throws up and the house smells."

"Let's hide our Sunday School shoes," someone suggested.

"We do that all the time. That's no fun."

"We could mess up the refrigerator."

"Why do we have to do that? Mom messes it up every day. That's not new."

"I know. We could tell grandma that mama drinks coffee and talks on the telephone all day and lets us run wild."

"Good idea. You can cry and act pitiful when she rushes over." The designated crier puffed up with pride and laid back on her pillow to practice wailing.

"One of us could paint the garage black and blame it on the neighbor kids."

"Write that one down. I think that's a winner."

"I've always wanted to leave Dad's tools out in the snow to rust," a son said shyly. A gasp went through the room.

"I don't think it's worth it," our oldest child warned. "We'd have to stay in our rooms for the rest of our lives."

"Does anyone know any new dirty words?" The kindergartner said she'd heard a couple.

"Those aren't new. They've been around as long as Thumbkins. Let me tell you what my teacher said when no one showed up for PTA. We can use it when the folks have important company." Everyone clapped!

"We could have Augie bite the mailman."

"He already did that last month, remember? And mom cried for two hours because the post office called and canceled our home delivery and made daddy get a box downtown. We don't want to make mom cry!" Everyone agreed that making mom cry wasn't much fun because daddy almost always took her out to eat and they had to stay home and have hot cereal for supper.

"I know what we could do. Let's all grow six inches so we'll have to have new school clothes."

"Fine for you buddy, but I get your dumb hand-me-downs. I don't like that idea."

"We can pretend that Barbie is pregnant and has to marry

126

Ken."

"How did that happen?" our five year old asked.

That's when I told them they could all get up from their naps if they wanted to. As far as I could see too much sleep can be a bad thing...I don't care what my mother said.

"BREAKING FAMILY TRADITION"

For the first time in 23 years one of our sons will miss Thanksgiving dinner at home. When I mentioned this to him on the telephone the other night I did not hear any heaving sobs. If you really want to know the truth I heard giggling in the background. High-pitched feminine giggling. I do not think he was giving his all to our conversation. I think he had something else on his mind..and I'm not sure that it was turkey and pumpkin pie.

"But he is so far away from home," I said to my husband. Tears sat on the edge of my eyelids. "And he has never basted a turkey in his life. He probably doesn't even know you have to baste. He will probably let it dry up."

"He may not even buy one," my husband reminded gently. "Turkey for one person is not very practical. You know how he feels about leftovers and there are very few two pound turkeys walking about."

I certainly did remember how he felt about leftovers. Most of our children grew up accepting the fact they were eating yester-say's meatloaf disguised as today's beef stroganoff. I figured if I gave it a fancy name and threw in some of last week's noodles I could fool them. But not our oldest son. He could sniff a used noodle the minute he walked into the kitchen.

"I've seen that noodle before," he would say, peering into the pot. "It definitely looks shabby." And he simply wouldn't eat it.

I suppose this is one of the reasons why he always enjoyed Thanksgiving dinner so much. He knew I started out fresh. He knew that I would not hustle forsaken food on a holiday. And, now, for the first time he was going to miss out on the thrill of sharing in all that good food and family fun.

When I made that statement our son-in-law raised his eyebrow. Down deep, I think he rather envied him. He has eaten eight or nine Thanksgiving dinners with us and he still isn't used to finding walnut shells in his whipping cream. He is nice about it but I can tell. I saw the expression on his face the year he chipped his front tooth. I offered to pay his dental bill but he just sighed and said "No."

"I hope he is not alone," I said wiping off a runaway teardrop. "No one should be alone."

"I don't think he will be alone," my husband grinned. He, too, had heard the giggling in the background.

"But it won't be the same," I said.

No, it won't be the same. I guess nothing ever is. Where else will he find a dog who waits patiently in the corner for the card-table leg to buckle under its load of platters and plates so he can claim his own.

Where else will he find a mother who puts the turkey in the automatic dryer to defrost to keep it from being sampled by the family cat as it is thawing?

Where else will he find a father whose veins stood out three inches when the mother forgot to put the turkey in the dryer?

Where else will he find a family cat who hides in the drain pipe on the side of the house when the first of November rolls around and stays there until the middle of January. A black family cat that has a good memory and snow-white hair?

Where else will he find little sisters that make colorful place mats out of toilet paper and a brother who produces strange noises during the prayer?

Where else will he find a grandfather who knows the batting average of every baseball player since 1925 and annually recites them through two helpings of mashed potatoes straight down to seconds on minced pie and an aunt who thinks he is the greatest ever and proves it by loaning him money?

Where else will he find big sisters who, at one time, changed his diapers and therefore are not impressed with his new, adult professional business title?

Where else will he find little nieces and nephews who look at him in awe because he is so much taller than they are and has a deep voice, occasionally tosses them in the air in merriment and/or growls at them when they block out his view of the kick-off?

Where else will he find a harvest table that looks as if it has a nervous headache and a mother who actually has a nervous headache because she has been in the kitchen since 4 a.m. and thus has broken a year-long habit of spending as little time in this particular room as possible? And, if everyone doesn't leave her alone and quit asking when the turkey is going to be done and has she put onions in the dressing and did she forget to sugar the cranberries again this year and why does the apple salad look brown she is just going to make reservations at a good restaurant next year and that is that.

Where else will he find a family that really does love him very much and will miss him terribly and the only thing that might get us all through the day with a smile and a warm feeling is calling him to wish him Happy Thanksgiving and hearing him say...

"I'll be home for Christmas!"

"HOLIDAY HOME DECORATOR"

It is time to decorate the house for Christmas. Hurrah! - Humbug!

The fact that I have limited talents in this direction doesn't alter my determination in any way. Along about the last of November when the leftover turkey is beginning to turn green right before my eyes. I begin to plan the elaborate and expensive decorations I am going to produce for Christmas.

"This year I am going to create!" I exclaimed to my family as I came up glassy-eyed from poring over pages and pages of "how-to's" in various women's magazines. They make it look so easy.

"Don't throw away any egg cartons, glass jars, colored string, thumb tacks, soap flakes, moth balls, cardboard, glue, bits of felt, toothpaste tubes, aluminum foil, feathers, cereal boxes or gum wrappers," I warn. "You may be getting rid of a potential angel."

"Please, we aren't going through the toothpick tree bit again, are we?" one of the boys asked, rolling his eyes in pure agony. He remembers the traumatic experience of being an innocent child and running barefoot through a house with a carpet that had suddenly spouted 3,789 toothpicks.

"What's a toothpick tree?" one of the little girls questioned.

"Don't ask!" my husband shuddered.

"Remember how the dog choked when he ate it? And threw up all over Dad's new shotgun that was under the Christmas tree?" Everyone laughed heartily at this memory. Everyone laughed but Dad, that is.

"Make a toothpick tree, Mom, it sounds like fun," begged the youngest child, whose memory had not been fully developed during this exciting period.

"Not this year," I said. "There's a shortage of toothpicks." She believed me. She also believes there is a shortage of sugar-coated cereals, plastic whistles, kittens-to-give-away-to-good-homes and money. And she believes that the President of the United States has personally sent me a signed document asking me not to provide any more of these items in our home. But that's another story.

For many years I have lived as the only lady in the neighborhood whose house looks little different at Christmas time than it does on the Fourth of July. I try. I try. I honestly do. We had a neighbor who could make something fantastic out of anything. Give her an old ball of twine, a rusty nail and a can of spray paint and Viola!...a glittering Christmas Star. Three or four rubber bands, seven corks and a cardboard box and she came up with one of the most beautiful Nativity scenes I have ever seen.

I thought to myself, "If she can do it...so can I!" The current kindergartner took one look at my creation and said, "Why do you have those three rubber bands and seven corks standing on the mantle in a cardboard box?" I threw the whole mess away.

In fact, I didn't speak to my neighbor again until sometime in February when I went over to find out how she made those pretty pink hearts out of coffee grounds and popcorn. I wouldn't let the children visit her either. I warned them if they stayed at her house very long they would end up a centerpiece.

Oh yes, I have plans for our Christmas decorations, but, alas, they won't work out. They never do. And I'll resort again to the bleach bottle turned Christmas candle that our Cub Scout made, lo those many years ago; Christmas stockings cut with pinking shears, that have dark places where the glue soaked through; the white cellophane wreath wrapped around a rusty clothes -hanger; dozens of styrofoam balls plunged into tons of glitter that spray showers of sparkles all over the house everytime someone opens the front door; silhouetted, multiple amputeed Santas dancing on the end of sewing thread, and pine cones that have been nibbled by mice.

And our old and somewhat battered Nativity scene. No matter that Joseph's face is slightly chewed or one of the sheep stands solidly by the manger with no head or the cow has lost her leg or the angel runs around with ragged wings.

It takes a hard mother not to soften just a little when she notices that Baby Jesus is fading in places because of so many kisses.

Perhaps that is why a mother's face eventually fades too.

"I NEED YOU, MR MAILMAN"

"What in heaven's name are you doing?" my husband asked coming into the room where I was sitting, both eyes peeled out the front window. "Are you watching the people across the street eat breakfast again? You know how they hate that."

"I'm waiting for the mailman." I said.

"He won't be here for another four or five hours. I hope you're not going to waste an entire morning just sitting there. If you'd try real hard, I bet you could find something constructive to do around the house while you're waiting." And he glanced up at a platoon of soldier spiders holding maneuvers on the ceiling by the chandelier.

Actually, I don't feel waiting for the mailman is a waste of time. I've done it for years. His arrival is the highlight of the day. True, quite often the only thing he brings is the electric bill or an advertisement for encyclopedias but nevertheless, I can always hope for something better. I've gotten over expecting a mash note from Paul Newman or an invitation from the White House but I still trust that occasionally I will get some personal mail. With the Christmas holidays approaching...surely someone will write to me. Maybe even you!

I can remember when the mailman thought coming to our house was more exciting than a trip to the moon. He never did know what to expect when he stepped one foot upon our porch and plunged his hand into our box. What a thrill it must have been to draw back his hand with 14 sticky suckers clinging to his fingertips. Or a dead frog; a wet mitten; a toddler's training pants kicked off in a moment of urinary weakness. That must have been quite a surprise! Once he told me he'd found an unstamped love letter from our six year old daughter to the boy next door. "Dere Mistur Maleman," it said. "Please take this letter to Jimmy. I luv Him." The fact the little note writer had hand-drawn the stamp instead of purchasing it from Uncle Sam didn't keep this kind man from delivering it to Jimmy. He even waited for an answer but Jimmy couldn't write. In fact Jimmy couldn't read either. Jimmy was a real dope and eventually grew up to be a very rich man. Much to everyone's surprise.

That kind mailman had an awful lot of patience with our children often making his rounds with half-a-dozen pre-schoolers trotting at his heels begging for letters. Perhaps he had a little less patience with Augie-Doggie who hid in our hedge and sprang out like a mad wolf whenever he saw a blue suit approach. Have you ever seen a mailman run with his mouth open? I have. One day he warned me that if I wanted any more electric bills and/or encyclopedia brochures I danged well better keep that ferocious animal tied up or locked inside the house. "You know I don't have to come here," he said.

"But I need you, Mr. Mailman," I wanted to beg. Instead, I quietly nodded my head and warned Augie if he chased that poor man one more time I was selling him to a circus.

Then we moved to the country, had a rural box by the road and the mailman drove a car instead of walking and Augie discovered chasing an automobile was much different, and much more taxing on his dog heart, than running after someone who only had two long legs and a heavy sack and growing tired of attacking steel, he soon gave it up as a bad job and turned all of his attention to the pigs across the road and drove them crazy instead. I stood by the door and watched for dust clouds on the country road and listened to my husband complain that I thought nothing of hopping a half a mile for the mail but balked at walking into the kitchen to get him a cold beer from the refrigerator. "How can you get so excited about someone that delivers bills?" he asked.

He doesn't always deliver bills, I told him. Sometimes he brings a letter from an old friend...a wedding invitation or a birth announcement from someone I didn't even know was married. And once in awhile the wedding invitation and birth announcement show up in the same envelope. Now THAT is exciting! Frequently I get advertisements for items that make my eyes grow big and round. "Oh my goodness," I said to my husband when I removed the plain brown wrapper. "Did you ever see anything like this before?" My husband just grinned.

I grow very restless on Sunday when the mailman takes his well-deserved rest and the day goes by on turtle feet. I can hardly stand it. Why I remember when he made two trips each day to our house. That was as close to heaven as I'll probably ever get. And I've often thought I should do something nice for him for a change because he's brought me so many years of pleasure. "Perhaps," I said thoughtfully, "I'll make him a nice batch of Christmas cookies."

"Please, don't, mom," our daughter said. "We'd have the Feds on our backs, for sure, and they might even cancel home deliveries altogether..and then where would you be?" Well, I couldn't stand that.

But I'm warning all of you right now...unless I get a lot of holiday letters I'm whipping up a batch of my special salty divinity and I'm going to pass a portion out to postoffices all over America and none of you are going to get any mail this Christmas either because your mailman probably won't be feeling up to par. And in the meantime I'm going to hunt up good old Jimmy's address, write him a sweet note and see if he'll loan me a little money so that I can get my Christmas shopping started.

By the way, just in case you wondered. My address is 1409 9th St., Aurora, NE. 68818. But I warn you right now I don't loan money!

"QUIET CHAIR IS ALWAYS BUSY"

I looked at the calendar. Wow! It's two weeks before Christmas.

I still have a million things to do. I'm trusting the Lord and my husband to help me accomplish some of them. Of course, I've ruled out any assistance with writing holiday letters, changing sheets and shooing spiders out of the bathrooms. My husband said the first thing he had to do was go to the bank and hope they were nice.

I have to figure out what I'm going to do with all the strange stuff I have in the cupboard. I bought all of these weird ingredients in early November so I could make exotic Christmas cookies and surprise family and friends.

I poured over recipes named Heavenly Bars, Nutty Carrot-Lemon Drops and delicate Oatmeal Lace Wafers. They sounded and looked so good. I'd planned about 49 different varieties (twelve dozen each) and stocked up on enough supplies to open my own bakery.

Neatly lining the dried apricots and pounds of hazelnuts on the shelves, I pushed aside last years oriental noodles and mandarin oranges. With good intentions, I pledged to use everything down to the last crumb.

So far, all I've managed to get rid of is a package of chocolate chips and a small bottle of red sprinkles. Anybody know a good, swift cookie recipe that calls for oriental noodles and dried apricots?

The next thing I must do is revise my Christmas buying. Getting a jump on things I asked our six-year-old grandson what he wanted for Christmas. This was in October.

"Oh, I want a dump truck, grandma," he said breathlessly.

Great. I went out and bought the largest, most colorful dump truck in the toy store. Setting it in the closet, I congratulated myself with being on top of things.

Two days ago I casually mentioned "dump truck."

"Yuck, grandma," he said. "No one has a dump truck. I want a radio controlled off-road vehicle with a working winch."

I asked my husband if he thought our 28-year-old son would be satisfied with a dump truck instead of the electric razor he'd asked for. He said he didn't think so.

Between now and the 24th I must dust off our "quiet chair." It's a very important part of that family time before we open gifts on Christmas Eve. Everyone knows that for a child (and sometimes for grandma) these hours stretch into an eternity.

The "quiet chair" was invented the year one of our granddaughters carefully measured every package under the tree and came up with the conclusion that she had the smallest gifts of all.

"Everybody else has a big present." She wailed and stomped. "Mine are all bitty."

Her older sister, whose tiniest gift was about 24x24, looked smug.

Lower lip down to her knees, she pouted and hung her head. Before I could say "grandma will run downtown and get a refrigerator box if you'll only smile," she was whisked off into the kitchen by her mother. Her little feet didn't even touch the floor. A stern lecture, accompanied by finger pointing, was going on when I arrived at the scene. My goodness, who would scold a child on Christmas Eve? Not in my house.

I gave her mother a dirty look, took our granddaughter gently by the hand and led her to the "quiet" corner. I gave her a candy cane and told her this was a "Special" chair for pretty people. I also pledged from that moment on anything she received, even if it was a page of stickers, would be wrapped in the largest box known to man.

Ten minutes later the "quiet chair" was occupied by our grandson, who'd grown tired of waiting and was not only opening his own gifts...but mine, his aunts, uncles and several cousins.

He was followed by his sweet sister who'd been sitting patiently in a corner, her presents carefully laid out around her. She'd been behaving very graciously until a smaller cousin had crawled over and attempted to touch one of her precious presents. Two flying fists had discouraged such prying. The "quiet chair" seemed a safe alternative.

Laura Elizabeth's turn came later. "One does not eat a Christmas tree, sweetheart," I explained as I picked her up from beneath it's branches where she was contentedly chewing on an expensive glitter-gold family heirloom.

Our two grown sons were threatened with being strapped in...together...when full of Christmas cheer, they teased a younger sister until she cried.

"But it's traditional, mom," They said when I objected. "It won't seem like Christmas Eve unless she bawls."

"Stop it right now!" I shouted.

"My goodness, mother," the finger shaking mama said. "Who would scold a child on Christmas Eve?"

Yesterday I told my husband he was just going to have to help me bake a fruit cake (adding dried apricots and oriental noodles if necessary); go to the store and buy an off-road vehicle with working winch and carry in the heavy carton I'd pasted together for our granddaughter's small necklace. "While you're at it," I said, "you can put the family heirloom ornament on top of the tree."

He said "No thank you, I'm going to sit down and watch a football game."

Maybe I'll have to drag out the "Quiet Chair" a few days early. There's no hardfast rule that prohibits grandpas from sitting there too.

"MISSING THE AFTER-CHRISTMAS CLEAN UP"

Twenty-one years ago I pulled off one of the most brilliant coups in the history of motherhood. I left home the day after Christmas!

No...I didn't take an extended trip to Hawaii or maintain a secret rendevouz with a handsome admirer. I simply went to the hospital to have a baby.

A desperate way to get out of taking down the Christmas tree, you say...well, you're right of course, but frankly the cause had been predetermined long before that...it was the timing that had to be exactly right.

Naturally, I didn't want to miss the excitement of Santa, Christmas Eve at Grandma's, Angel Choirs (full of MY Angels) and eating all that yummy sugary stuff. In truth, I was already so fat one more pound or two of fudge wasn't going to hurt..or show. My due date had come and gone and my doctor had thrown up his hands, walked about the examining room and muttered something about medical school not preparing him for "Tweedle-dee-dee" in maternity clothes. I'd warned him for weeks I had no intentions of missing Christmas-at-home with my family no matter what he said or what the stork wanted.

And I sat throughout that entire Christmas Day with my legs crossed, trying to ignore the funny little tingly sensations running up and down my spine, determined not to give into nature but to stick it out until the last light on our Christmas tree dimmed. Too tired to even think about a trip to the hospital, I lumped into bed that night and dreamed I had given birth to a child with a large and blinking red nose.

In nearly everyone's house the day after Christmas is well-known as a definite anti-climax. It's the day when "someone" has to be brave and face up to the ground-in peanut brittle in the carpet, non-existant 3-D batteries, the thank you notes to be written and soothing the preschooler whose gift had been burned up when Dad fired the crumpled wrapping paper in the incinerator. At our house (and I'm sure, yours too) that "someone" is mother. A tired mother. Who harbored the secret urge to strangle Frosty the Snowman with his woolen scarf if he so much as squealed one more musical note.

On that particular December 26th I heaved myself out of bed at 6:30 a.m. to settle 18 quarrels over a monopoly game; pried two rubber darts from between a startled Augie's eyebrows; spent 45 futile and precious minutes hunting for a tiny Barbie doll bra and listened to a chorus of children, surrounded by $2,000 worth of Christmas toys whining in unison "What's there to do? I'm bored!" I knew exactly what to do. I went directly to the telephone, called my husband at the office and said "Come home! It's time to go to the hospital!"

"Now?" he said. "I'm on my coffee break. We're having fruit-cake."

"Now!" I yelled. "Call Grandma."

"Do you have pains?" he asked.

"By the time you get here...I will have," I promised firmly.

When I called the doctor he said he knew I'd pull something like this since it was the first time in 20 years he'd had a two day vacation. Picking up my suitcase, I stood by the door with my coat on, waiting for my husband to drive in the driveway and I looked at the chaos around me and knew that it wasn't going to make one iota of difference if all the Tinkertoys were lost or a brand new Teddy bear tumbled into the potty chair or that, Auntie-dear finally showed up to claim her present only to find our second son had broken into the box and eaten all the good chocolates. I wasn't going to be there. Hallelujah! I had other important stuff to do.

Our sixth child was born that day..and very quickly, too, I might add. One glance at the faces of both my husband and my doctor convinced me that I should probably try and manage a fast delivery. The nurses, on the other hand, were showing some real joy. Most of them were mothers, too, and happy as heck to be anywhere but home on the day-after Christmas. They stood around the room congratulating me, each other and anyone who cared to listen.

Our lovely new daughter weighed nearly nine pounds and the doctor grinned, touched her softly on the cheek and said "If your mother had kept you hidden much longer, sweetheart, you could've walked into the nursery all by yourself."

My husband seemed very proud and swore it was well worth missing fruitcake to have such a fine baby girl. The fact she looked exactly like him helped a lot, too, I believe.

Having done such a startling day's work in a pretty short time, I settled back on my pillow and thoroughly rested, relaxed and relished that entire hospital stay, managing just the exact amount of pitiful expression and weakness to convince the doctor I should probably stay right where I was until our older children went back to school and the Christmas tree was safely down at home.

True, the next year when I unpacked our ornaments in preparation to putting up the tree I found nearly half were crushed, some were smeared with peanut butter and the Angel who stood on top of our tree was missing her left eye. A large note was prominently tacked on a string of lights...it read "Don't EVER Do This To Me Again." signed "Your Husband!" I suppressed the urge to ask him Who Did What to Whom and smiled to myself.

I didn't smile, however, when I unpacked my suit case at the hospital and found the only underwear I'd brought was a tiny Barbie Doll bra.

"IT'S BEEN OUR PLEASURE"

Dear Children:

Your daddy is asleep, I can hear him snoring. It's so wintery cold outside, maybe you can hear him too. Isn't it a glorious sound? It's like the ringing of holiday bells. It means he's safe...he's well...he's warm...and he belongs to us! Aren't you glad I found him? You should be. For if I hadn't, you wouldn't be sitting next to your own Christmas trees in your own homes. Of course, I did have some small part in your creation. I realize it's hard to imagine such a thing. Trust me! It's true.

Perhaps you've noticed that your parents are mellowing out a bit as we grow older. But this doesn't keep us from thinking the world would be perfect if we could've kept all of you forever young...innocent...dependent...unhurt and never having to face the hard knocks of reality. But we realized you were growing up when you stopped bringing home your dirty laundry each time you came for a visit. As much as we loved you when you were little-we admire you as adults.

It was a twist of fate that you happened to be around when I learned my lessons of motherhood. I wish that I could've learned a few of them on someone else. It would've been a lot easier on you had I practiced my ranting and ravings on strangers. I guess I thought if I stomped and screamed you'd remember. I can only hope it's the smiles you kept in mind.

Tonight, I take the time to look back on some of those smiles. The Christmas, for instance, when I pretended awe and surprise at being handed an already-licked candy cane as a special gift for Mommy.

Wrapped in crumpled paper and stuck together with a complete roll of scotch tape, it took me 15 minutes to open the package. The eyes, suspensefully watching were so bright and hopeful I didn't dare admit that my stomach cramped at the thought of actually eating such a gift, but I swallowed every bite and tried to ignore the tiny bits of unidentifiable fluff clinging to it's sticky surface.

Your gift giving has become much more sophisticated but quite often, Lord, I long for just one more candy cane.

Remember the year when one of you sadly came to me and said "Look mommy, naughty Rudolph went potty under the Christmas tree." Not wanting to destroy a child's illusion, I quietly cleaned it up and just as quietly took down Augie-doggie's stocking and replaced the dog chewies with black coal. Following such incidents, I sometimes thought it would be much easier for your father and I to sail to Hawaii for the holidays.

Five minutes after I started decorating those funny ginger-bread men, I knew I should've tossed that tradition out the window. I was going to give it up this year. Last week, I received a call from Minneapolis..."Have you made the boys' yet Mom?" I hauled out the cookie tins and got to work. Hawaii would have to wait for another time...another year.

We'll probably never know what special "Baby Angel" sat upon her star and said "We'll give Lee and Shirley Lueth this baby and that baby," ultimately doling out seven. There were days when I wanted to wring her neck. You'll be glad to know, however, there were days that I was more grateful than words can tell. Especially at Christmas time. What a joy to watch as each of you found your secret wishes under our tree. And when the day was over, beneath the junk of wrappings, ribbons and tinsel, the warmth we'd shared couldn't be whisked away by a mere vacuum cleaner.

As I sit here remembering, it never really mattered that Augie peeved about finding black coal instead of his chewies, ate the artificial snow and threw up on the floor; that when the seven of you sat in a circle playing "hot potato" someone always lost and accused the others of cheating; that your daddy often drifted away for a nap in his big chair when the noise level reached a science-fiction pitch. How he could sleep has always been one of the universal mysteries of all time. By the way, he can still do it.

There was never enough privacy, never enough closet space, never enough money but always there was more than enough caring and love. You simply had to look for it at times. But it was definitely there and if you didn't find it, alas, it was because you didn't search hard enough. I'm happy to say, it's still here. We'll find it again this Christmas. Again I say...Trust me!

When we get together this Christmas Eve we can turn back the clock and the six-foot son will be a small boy again, handing me a candy cane wrapped in crushed paper; a mature daughter, a mother herself, will give me a certain smile, eyes dancing, and I'll know we're still on the same wave-length; a business-like son will clear his throat look manly and say "I had a cold last week, Mommy. I was sick." I'll use my usual cure...a soft hug and he'll be well; the Minneapolis daughter will find her special gingerbread man and when she nibbles, she'll be three years old again; the tickle in our giggle-tree kid will do some off-the-wall thing, like mash the potatoes in the blender because logically it should save time...realistically it jammed the blender, and we know that even if she can't cook, she can still make us all laugh; the in-laws mingle so well, we don't recognize them as in-laws...they simply become our children, too; five precious little girls and one sturdy, handsome little boy bring back memories of yesterday with a tug of the heart that's so sweet it sometimes hurts and our youngest daughter will confirm our faith that when we finally wound it all up and said "This is it," we really did it royally.

We're glad we chose to be your parents. It's been our pleasure. Merry Christmas...Mom and Dad.